A Guide to
EDINBURGH'S COUNTRYSIDE

A Guide to
EDINBURGH'S COUNTRYSIDE
Habitats and Walks within the City Boundary

Edinburgh Natural History Society

Macdonald Publishers, Edinburgh

To IAN and MARY SIME
who over the years passed on
so much enthusiasm, knowledge and wisdom
to members of the
EDINBURGH NATURAL HISTORY SOCIETY

The publication of this book has been made possible by the financial assistance of the Carnegie United Kingdom Trust.

Designed and edited by Jenny Carter

Published by
Macdonald Publishers
Loanhead
Midlothian
EH20 9SY

ISBN 0904 265 82 X (cased)
      0904 265 83 8 (paperback)

Printed in Scotland by
Macdonald Printers (Edinburgh) Ltd
Edgefield Road
Loanhead
Midlothian
EH20 9SY

Contents

Acknowledgements

The members of the Committee responsible for the production of this book would like to thank all those who have contributed or given advice. They are grateful to the Planning Department of Edinburgh District Council for their help and co-operation and for allowing reference to be made to the Department's maps when those for the book were being drawn.

Map for Walks 3a and 3b

The map for Walks 3a and 3b has been drawn with the kind agreement of the owner of the sheep-grazing land over which the walks pass. Dogs should always be kept on a leash.

Walk 4

We are grateful to Heriot-Watt University for allowing Walk 4 to pass through the University Campus.

Cemeteries

Note by G. D. C. Walker, District Ecologist.

Cover Photograph

Photograph of a roadside verge in the Balerno area taken by an amateur member of the Edinburgh Natural History Society.

Foreword

One of the problems of the twentieth century is that more and more people have come to live within the towns, or at least within the confines of the urban sprawl. Without doubt this can have the effect of cutting them off from the countryside and perhaps alienating them from the vital cause of conservation which may appear to pertain only to that other landscape, the countryside.

Hooray! Here is a book which not only shows that there is much of natural history interest within the confines of a great city, but that it is part of that wider countryside which both reaches into and out from the completely man-made environment.

From its foundation in volcanic rocks, its recent history held in peat, through its flora and fauna to its people, the City of Edinburgh is depicted as a vibrant living thing full of fascination. Here is a story well told and well worth reading. The walks will lead you from its past through its present to a brighter future, for it must engender in its readers that sense of conservation both for the semi-natural and the man-made aspects of this Great City.

During the hey-day of Natural History it was the local Societies that led the way and recorded the local facts for posterity. It is great to see the Edinburgh Natural History Society continuing to play that role by taking this initiative for the future.

The book will be of great use to residents and visitors alike and I can specially recommend it to teachers, a nature reserve complete with trails right on your own front door.

Edinburgh has always been one of my favourite cities—now I know why.

David J. Bellamy

Bedburn
October 1981

Preface

The Edinburgh Natural History Society, now over 100 years old, was founded in 1869 as the Edinburgh Naturalists Field Club. Later the name was changed to the Edinburgh Field Naturalists and Microscopical Society, while its present name was taken in 1921 when the Society merged with the Scottish Natural History Society.

The aim of the Society is the enjoyment of natural history which does not mean that it is averse to scientific outlook and professional expertise for it is aware that enjoyment of any branch of natural history is enhanced when knowledge is more than superficial.

In spite of the growth of the City, Edinburgh remains particularly rich in natural history interest with its hills and moorland, rivers, reservoirs and ponds, woods, quarries and a shoreline all within easy reach of the townsman and visitor by local public transport.

It is hoped that, with the help of this book, many will have greater understanding and enjoyment of the many and varied habitats which help to make Edinburgh such an attractive City.

Many members of the Society have contributed to the book by making observations, choosing routes, identifying plants and animals, drawing maps and illustrating what may be seen on the walks. Although the walks are planned to cover the many habitats, what is emphasised on each walk varies with the type of habitat and the special interests of the writers.

The Society wishes to record its thanks to the Carnegie United Kingdom Trust whose generous financial aid and interest made this publication possible.

Introduction

1: The Environment of Edinburgh

During the last 300 years or so much valuable recording of plants, animals and rocks has been carried out. Today the study of Natural History involves not only recording but also the study of relationships between plants and animals including Man and the relationships of plants and animals to their environment.

Animals and plants live together in places called habitats. These may be of any size, for example, a moor, a forest or wood, a quarry or cliff, a tree, a wall or garden path, even a log, all can be studied as a habitat. The smaller ones, such as a tree or log, are usually spoken of as micro-habitats.

By this booklet it is hoped to introduce readers in a very simple way to the major habitats which may be seen in walks through Edinburgh and District. It sets out to be illustrative, *not* comprehensive. To help understand background information in the description of the walks some notes on the formation of landscape are given in the first chapter. For the Geology of the Edinburgh area readers should refer to *The Geology of the Lothians and South East Scotland* edited by G. Y. Craig and P. McL. D. Duff, Scottish Academic Press, 1975.

It is thought that at an early stage the earth was a spinning globe of molten material, some of which on cooling formed a crust of crystalline rocks, known as *igneous rocks*. In the hot mass there must have been water vapour, which on cooling condensed to form the water of the lakes and seas partly covering the crust. The surface of the rocks exposed to the atmosphere would have been broken up or weathered and the fragments produced carried away by wind, water and ice. Later these would have been laid down in horizontal layers or strata under water forming the first *sedimentary rocks*. By movements of the earth's crust in time many of these would have become raised above the water. The wearing down or weathering of rocks, both igneous and sedimentary, has been a continuous process and is still going on today, so forming new rocks.

After the initial cooling, molten material or magma still existed in the depths of the earth's crust. At times at points of weakness in the crust it found its way to the surface, sometimes reaching it and being ejected through volcanoes as lava or volcanic ash (tuff) or else thrusting itself between layers of sedimentary rocks to form

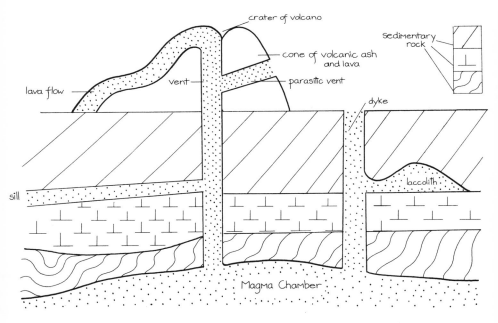

Figure 1:   The Formation of Igneous Rocks

intrusions of igneous rocks (see Figure 1). Molten material contains many minerals. On cooling above ground or in the crater as a plug or vent it forms igneous rocks such as basalt, a dark heavy-looking crystalline rock whose crystals cannot be seen without a microscope; sponge-like rocks such as pumice stone; and agglomerate which consists chiefly of volcanic ash cemented into solid rock. Granite is an example of an igneous rock which has formed by much slower cooling underground. The crystals in it can be seen without a microscope.

Sometimes movements of the earth's crust have caused cracks and fractures in the laid down rocks followed by their displacement. The lines along which the rocks move are called faults. In Scotland, two large faults, the Highland Boundary Fault and the Southern Boundary Fault separate the lower ground of the Central area in which Edinburgh lies from higher land to the north and to the south. Not all faults are as large as these two boundary ones and smaller ones in the Edinburgh area will be pointed out in Walk 1.

Sedimentary rocks in the Edinburgh area

Sedimentary rocks which help to form the scenery of Edinburgh

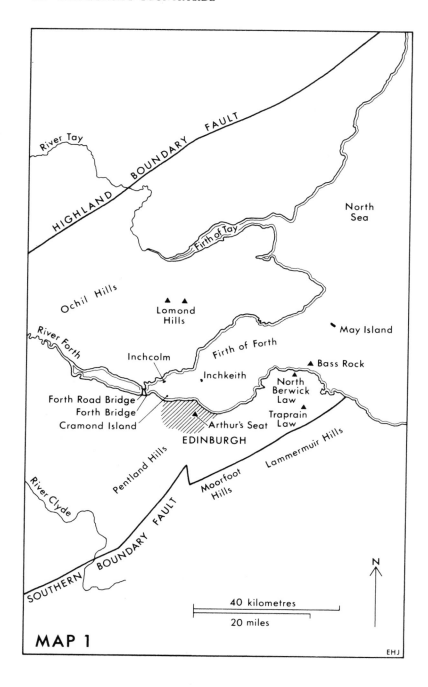

North
Sea

River Tay

HIGHLAND   BOUNDARY   FAULT

Firth of Tay

Ochil Hills

Lomond
Hills

May Island

River Forth

Firth of Forth

Inchcolm

Inchkeith

Bass Rock

North
Berwick
Law

Forth Road Bridge
Forth Bridge
Cramond Island

Arthur's Seat

Traprain
Law

EDINBURGH

Pentland Hills

Lammermuir Hills

River Clyde

Moorfoot
Hills

SOUTHERN   BOUNDARY   FAULT

N

40 kilometres

20 miles

MAP 1

EHJ

and District were laid down over a very long period 400-250 million years ago. The commonest are the sandstones and the shales.

Sandstones are rocks made up of the laid down sand grains which have become cemented together. Sometimes they contain calcium carbonate (limestone) derived from the shells of marine animals which lived in the sea when the rocks were forming and then they are known as calciferous sandstones. Examples of sandstones will be pointed out on the Arthur's Seat Walk and on the Cramond Walk. Much of the stone used in the building of Edinburgh's New Town is of the creamy coloured calciferous sandstone which was obtained from Craigleith Quarry.

Shales are formed of very fine particles of clay which become held together in layers to form solid rock. A rocky outcrop of shale will be pointed out on Walk 5. Figure 2 is of the steep gorge at

the Dean Bridge which exposes the Wardie shales with sandstones above them. Wardie shales are shales impregnated with compounds of hydrogen and carbon thought to have come from decaying plant debris.

Igneous activity and igneous rocks within the Edinburgh area

When the sedimentary rocks of the Edinburgh District were forming there was much igneous activity. The Arthur's Seat volcano became active about 340 million years ago. For most of its active life the cone was under water and the lava which poured out became interbedded with sedimentary rocks. (The extinct volcano called Arthur's Seat takes its name from the hill within Holyrood Park which forms only part of the volcano.)

Figure 2:   *The Steep Gorge at the Dean Bridge cut in the Wardie Shales by the post-glacial stream of the Water of Leith*

The extinct volcano which we know today must be very different in shape from the original one, for during the millions of years which have followed its active period, much of the soft volcanic ash forming the cones has become worn away leaving the vents. Much of the surrounding sedimentary rock has also been worn away. As a result what has been left of the volcano stands out and dominates the scenery of the Edinburgh area.

What remains of the volcano which can be seen on the walks, either at close quarters or from a distance consists of:

i) Five 'plugs' or vents—

Lion's Head Vent (see Figure 3) forming the summit crag of Arthur's Seat

Lion's Haunch Vent (see Figure 3)

Pulpit Rock Vent

Castle Rock (see Figure 5)

Crag Vent

ii) Portions of cone—

Whinny Hill, Calton Hill

iii) Lava flows—

Thirteen individual basalt lava flows, erupted from four vents, have been identified:

Lava I—from the Castle Rock Vent

II—from the Lion's Head Vent

III—from the Pulpit Rock Vent

IV—from the Lion's Head Vent

V-XIII—from the Lion's Haunch Vent

iv) A number of sills and dykes—

which have become exposed, e.g. the well-recognised sill of the basalt cliff-like Salisbury Crag (see Figure 3) which formed between sedimentary rocks after the volcano became extinct:

St Leonard's sill (see Figure 3)

Figure 3:

1. *Lion's Head Vent*   2. *Lion's Haunch Vent*
3. *Samson's Rib Intrusion*   4. *Salisbury Crags Sill*
5. *St Leonard's Sill*   6. *Crow Hill*

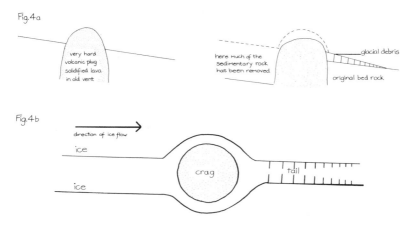

Figure 4:   Formation of Crag and Tail

The Ice Age and after

Much of the change in shape of Edinburgh's scenery mentioned in the last section must have come about during the Ice Age.

From about one million years ago to about 10,000 years ago, Britain was in the grip of intermittent glaciation. During this period the ice movement brought about moulding of the rocks. In the Edinburgh area the ice travelled eastward moving soft rock before it and grinding around and over hard rock lying in its path. For example, it ground around the hard basalt plug of the Castle rock cutting away the surrounding sedimentary rock except on the protected or lee side, producing what is known as the 'crag and tail' effect (see Figure 4a and 4b).The tail of sedimentary rock forms the ridge on which the Royal Mile was built (see Figure 5). Near the Portcullis gate of the Castle, visitors will see

the junction of the basalt plug of the crag with the grey sedimentary rock of the tail. The basalt plug passes through the floor of the War Memorial. Notice that the sides of the crag are very steep giving an almost impregnable position to the Castle and that on the north-west there are grooves or striae formed by ice movement.

The effect of ice movement on Arthur's Seat has been to produce westward facing crags with gentle slopes on their east side. Other 'crag and tail' effects include Blackford Hill (see Walk 2), Craiglockhart Hill and Calton Hill.

When the sedimentary rocks around the castle plug became cut away, a gorge—the Waverley Gorge—was formed to the north, and a depression which is now occupied by the Cowgate and Grassmarket to the south. The Waverley Gorge became a marshy-filled hollow, used as the artificial lake known as the Nor' Loch from

Figure 5:   *Crag and Tail. The hard volcanic rock of the Castle Hill acted as a bastion against the ice sheet advancing from the west. It protected the rock of the esplanade and the Royal Mile which remained as a 'tail' behind the 'crag' of the Castle Rock*

1450, when it was dammed up, until 1759. In that year drainage began in order to landscape the area as Princes Street Gardens.

St Margaret's Loch, man-made in 1856 in a marshy hollow formed by ice, and Duddingston Loch are two examples of glacial lochs which exist today, while the parkland of the Meadows was developed on the site of the post-glacial Burgh Loch. This, at one time, was a broad lake from which Edinburgh drew some of its water.

Other results of glaciation which will be pointed out on walks include raised beaches, deposits of boulder clay laid down when the ice melted, post-glacial outflow channels carved out either by melt waters or by a river when its pre-glacial valley has been blocked. An outflow channel caused by melt ice, mentioned in Walk 2, is the one which carried melt water from the valley of the Water of Leith above Colinton to Craigmillar by way of the Braid

Valley. An example of an outflow channel carved out by a river is the gorge in the Wardie Shale at Dean Bridge cut out by the Water of Leith when its pre-glacial channel became blocked (see Figure 2).

The Pentland Hills

Running south-west from the Edinburgh area the Pentland Hills, which at their northern end dominate the southern outskirts of the City, form a narrow belt of high ground. They are composed mainly of a complex mixture of sandstone and volcanic rocks. These along with other rocks underlying them, must have become arched up as a result of earth movement 300 or so million years ago to form the present range of hills. Much of the rock surface would have become worn away. The whole Pentland range was overridden with ice during the glaciation.

Two peaks — Caerketton (1550 feet/473 m) and Allermuir (1617 feet/492 m) — of volcanic origin which lie within the city area are included in the Pentland Walk. The Black Hill, an example of a lacolith (see Figure 1) with its smooth dome contrasting with the neighbouring craggy lava, can be seen south of the City Boundary.

Invasion of vegetation

After the ice had dwindled away vegetation spread through Britain — at first it was tundra-like. Then followed moorland plants — Heather, Arctic Willow, Deer Grass, Sphagnum Moss and many others. As the ground warmed up, trees — Birch, Hazel, Scots Pine, Juniper and Rowan — came in, followed later by the less hardy Oak, Ash, Elm and Alder.

All vegetation must have reached Scotland overland from the continent via England which was joined to the rest of Europe by a land bridge. Although there were many fluctuations, overall the weather continued to warm up and by 5000 BC most of the ice had melted. Britain became an island. A rapid spread of the already established trees followed,

the Oak becoming the dominant tree below 1000 feet (305 m) and the Scots Pine above.

We have been able to ascertain what vegetation colonised Britain in post-glacial times by examining fossil pollen grains preserved at different levels in peat which can be dated and which now covers the surface of boggy areas.

Peat is made up of plant remains only partly decomposed. It forms under water-logged conditions where there is little of the oxygen present necessary to support the micro-organisms which cause decay. Pollen grains of plants growing at the time of the peat formation become enveloped in the peat. By sinking tubes into the peat covering of a bog it is possible to extract samples from different levels and examine pollen grains. The outer wall of the grain is very resistant to decay and the characteristic pattern of its surface usually makes it possible to identify the species from which it comes. Only part of the pollen found in the peat is derived from flowering plants which must have grown on the bog. Much would have blown in from the surrounding country, so examining the peat gives an idea of the vegetation which once covered the whole area.

Figure 6:   Pentland Hills

There is no reason to think that the Edinburgh area was different from the rest of Britain. Investigations including those on deposits of peat in Corstorphine (which is now within Edinburgh) and in Holyrood Park at Hunter's Bog, point to there having been Oak forests wherever the land was suitable; lochs, marshes and bogs remaining in other places. There is evidence that trees reached the top of the Pentlands.

The last 7000 years

De-afforestation probably began as early as the Bronze Age. There is some evidence that a Bronze Age Settlement existed in Edinburgh near Duddingston, a large hoard of Bronze implements having been dredged out of Duddingston Loch. Certainly Iron Age Man must have cleared trees on the south and east slopes of Dunsappie to make space for their settlement. Cultivation terraces were made by building walls of stone and scratching the soil behind them. These, now 2000 years old, will be seen on the Arthur's Seat Walk.

Destruction of natural woodland continued over Britain through Roman and Saxon times and onwards through the Dark Ages. The pattern of de-afforestation in the Edinburgh area and surrounding country followed that of the rest of Britain. When the Romans—in AD 43 there was a Roman Fort at Cramond—carried out the first programme of land usage by cutting down forests or draining marshes and by road-making for troop movements, they must have cut down some of the Old Lothian Forest mentioned in the Hermitage Walk.

By the reign of James IV (1488-1513) felling to provide wood for shipbuilding was considerable and at that time forests around Edinburgh and Leith disappeared rapidly; although according to records the Burgh Muir, the land beyond the Burgh Loch, which stretched away to the hills of Blackford and Braid, remained covered with forest until much later. The land which became cleared was used for agriculture. The riverside villages along the Water of Leith, such as Stockbridge, which depended on water power for their mills, grew larger.

De-afforestation of natural woodland—woodland in which the trees have regenerated naturally without the help of Man—continued to the present century, and now in Britain there is very little natural forest left. In the Edinburgh area some traces are found along the steep banks of winding streams, such as the River Esk and its tributaries; in cleuchs in the Pentlands (odd Birches, Rowans, Willows, Juniper) and Pedunculate and Sessile Oaks and Ash on the Dalkeith Estate just outside the Edinburgh area. Until the end of the 18th century and the beginning of the 19th century, building in Edinburgh was restricted to the 'Crag and Tail' on which the building of the Castle had begun in the early Middle Ages. The building of the New Town took place at the end of the 18th century and the beginning of the 19th century on the agricultural land north of the 'Crag and Tail' and Nor' Loch. Later a second New Town to the north of the first, nearer to the sea, developed. In the mid-19th century Edinburgh expanded southwards to the edge of Blackford Hill.

Replanting of woodlands and amenity planting

By the end of the 17th century there had been some attempt at replanting woods, and as the land became taken over for agriculture trees were planted near steadings, in hedges round fields and in shelter areas. Land owners began planting trees on their private estates not only to provide timber and shelter for stock but to increase the attractiveness of the grounds, known as policies, of large estates and to provide privacy for large houses.

Growing in these policies are not only native trees—Scots Pine, Ash, Birch, Oak—but others which have been introduced from abroad, such as Beech, imported from England and used a great deal in shelter belts; Sycamore, which came from France in the 16th century and has now spread widely and Conifers such as Larches, Cypresses, Firs and the occasional Giant Sequoia or Wellingtonia. Undergrowth in these policies include Rhododendron species from Asia Minor, Cherry Laurel and Barberry from the Mediterranean, and Snowberry and Mahonia from North America. Also there are introduced herbaceous plants, e.g.

Few-flowered Leek, Pink Purslane and Yellow Figwort.

As soon as City Parks were made trees were planted in them, although the conditions of poor soil, brought about mainly by the annual destruction of dead leaves in the name of tidiness and much wind and pollution, are not congenial for their growth. The commonest trees are the relatively hardy Sycamore and English (Common) Elm. The latter is now under threat from Dutch Elm disease.

Map 2 shows the present extent of the Edinburgh District and the year in which each area was included in it. The environment is very varied including in addition to the normal urban features an extinct volcano; a trout stream flowing through the heart of the most built-up areas where Kingfishers may be seen; fifteen miles of coastline and two peaks of over 1000 feet (305 m). In the next chapter it will be shown that within its boundaries nearly every type of habitat for living things is represented.

Climate of Edinburgh

The climate of Edinburgh is typical of the east coast of Scotland. Annual rainfall is low, varying from 25 in. around Leith to 35 in. on the Pentland Hills (625 to 900 mm), compared with Glasgow's 40 in. (1000 mm) and some places in the western Highlands which experience 165 in. (4200 mm). Heavy rainfall is, however, a feature of the late summer, August or September

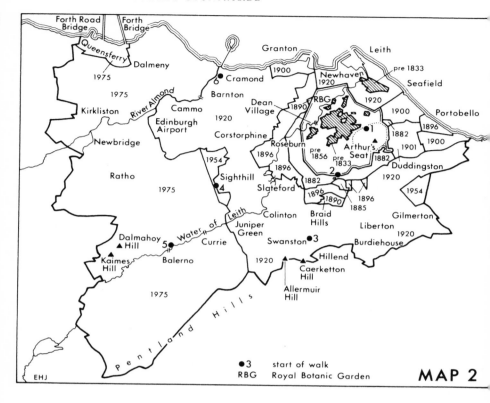

Map 2 shows the present extent of the Edinburgh District and the year in which each area was included in it. The start of each walk described in this book is also shown.

being often the wettest month of the year. Prolonged and severe thunderstorms are only rare events. Many of these reach the British Isles from France but rarely penetrate as far north as Scotland.

The district escapes extreme low temperatures because of the long sea track of easterly winds and the ameliorating influence of the Firth of Forth. Winter temperatures are thus comparable with those of London. The spring is often late and cool due to the slow rise of sea temperatures with the lengthening days. Robert Louis Stevenson described the climate with some justification as 'a downright meteorological purgatory in the spring'. Summer day-time temperatures tend to be 3°C (7°F) lower than southern England. The growing season is consequently shorter and average dates of flowering are approximately a fortnight later than London and three weeks later than Cornwall.

Sea fog, locally known as 'haar', ruins many potentially brilliant fine days in spring and early summer. It results from the moistening and cooling of warm air from the continent by the cold waters of the North Sea; Edinburgh residents are not comforted by the thought that their inland neighbours are probably basking in the warmth of cloudless skies only a few miles away.

The close proximity to the sea has a beneficial consequence in that prolonged snow cover is a feature of only a small minority of winters, although local frost hollows can produce micro-habitats differing significantly over distances measured in yards.

Nevertheless it should be remembered that Britain has the mildest climate at a comparable latitude anywhere in the world, because of the prevailing south-westerly wind directions over the warm waters of the Atlantic.

2: Habitats Within the City Boundary

Places where animals and plants live can be broadly divided into land, fresh water and salt water habitats in the following way:

Land habitats
Woodland
Grassland
Arable fields
Heathland and moorland
Hedgerows
Road verges
Built-up areas with parks and gardens
Wasteland

Inland water habitats

Burns or streams

Rivers

Canals

Lochs and reservoirs

Fens, marshes, bogs

Coastal water habitats

Sandy and muddy shores

Rocky shores and cliffs

Dunes

Salt marshes

Open water

Nearly all these habitats are represented in a patchwork-like way within the City Boundary. Animals that live in the built-up areas of a City Centre have become completely adapted to life alongside humans being sheltered by buildings and feeding on organic debris dropped by Man.

Most City inhabitants, however, although influenced by Man to a greater or lesser degree are similar to those found in the country outside the urban area. The animals and plants within them form a society or community in which animals are sheltered by the plants and depend on those with green colouring matter (chlorophyll) directly or indirectly for their food.

Green plants build up food (sugar, starch, proteins and fats) from simple raw materials — carbon dioxide which they take from the air, and water and mineral salts from the soil. The chlorophyll traps the sunlight which provides the energy needed. (The process in which carbohydrates are built up is known as photosynthesis.)

Animals' dependence on green plants for food can be illustrated by food chains, some examples of which are given below:

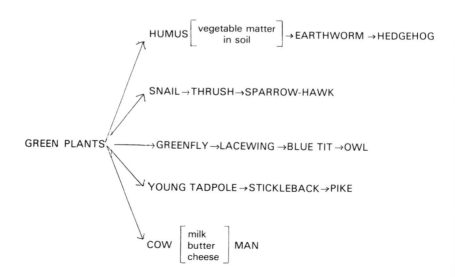

BARE ROCK ⟶ MOSSES AND LICHENS ⟶ GRASSLAND

GRASSLAND ⟶ SCRUB ⟶ WOODLAND

OPEN WATER ⟶ REED SWAMP ⟶ MARSH ⟶ SCRUB ⟶ WOODLAND

Examples of succession

It is not difficult to recognise much of the vegetation in a habitat although the ground flora varies with the season. Which animals are visible depends not only on the time of year but a great deal on the weather and the time of day or night. Mammals are particularly elusive, although you may be able to detect their presence by some sign, such as a fox's hole, faecal droppings, footprints, especially when the ground is covered with snow (see Figure 7, page 24).

The soil is an important part of most areas. Many soil organisms, e.g. Earthworms, Bacteria, Fungi, living within it bring about the breakdown or decay of dead animals and plants and in the process the minerals needed by green plants for protein manufacture are renewed.

Over the years communities change unless prevented from doing so through the activities of Man and grazing animals. Above are some examples of *succession*, the name given to this changing process.

For Britain woodland is the climax vegetation, the vegetation which is in equilibrium with our climate wherever the soil is suitable.

Some notes on Edinburgh's habitats, most of which may be seen on the walks, are now given.

Trees and woodlands

As pointed out in Chapter 1 there are many woodlands which have grown up over the years planted with a mixture of native and introduced species. Some of these will be passed through on the walks, for example at the Hermitage, beside the River Almond at Cramond and in the grounds of Riccarton estate. Other fine ones will be seen on Corstorphine Hill, in the Dean Valley and Colinton Dell through both of which the Water of Leith flows.

In the agricultural areas on the outskirts, groups of broadleaved trees and Conifers forming copses have been planted to form shelter belts or blocks. There are many on the slopes of the Pentlands including the cross-shaped T Wood, mainly of broad-leaved trees with a few Conifers, and the private plantation of European Larch passed on the Pentland Walk above Hillend.

At places there are self-sown trees, e.g. Alders at the side of

CAT

Four toes on each foot show without claw-prints, except where landing from a height, or after a leap.

RAT

Tracks show four toes at front and five toes behind. Short claw marks. Sometimes the drag of the tail shows.

SQUIRREL

Moves in hops. Look for four toes in front, and five behind, with a distinct heel mark. The claws show up, the the tracks appear in groups of four.

RABBIT

The hind feet leap-frog well in front of the front paws. Each leap may be a yard long. Front feet are five-toed, hind feet four-toed, the claws seldom show. Hare tracks are larger.

ROE DEER

Footprints or "slots" often found after rain or snow, or in soft ground. The doe "slot" usually points straight forward, the buck turns out his feet more.

HEDGEHOG

Largest of the British insectivores: fairly common except on high ground. Tracks are five-toed with claws. Prints of hind and fore-feet often overlap and the scratch marks of the spines may show.

MOLE

Claws on front feet are very pronounced. The hind feet show as normal five-toed tracks. Footprints are rare.

BADGER

Bar-like pad mark, five toes and long claws especially on the front feet. Top diagrams show a trotting trail. The bottom one the sort of footprint found at the badger sett.

FOX

Tracks about the same size as terrier dog. Four toes on each foot, ball of foot smaller and more rounded than a dog's, and claws are finer. At normal speed hind feet almost on print of the fore-feet

burns, Willows in most damp places; Downy Birch, Rowan, Willow, Hawthorn along the Pentland cleuchs, where animals cannot nibble; more Downy Birch on the rough grassland of the Pentlands where up to about 1200 feet (366 m) there are scattered Juniper plants, mostly low bushes rather than trees, thought to be the remains of the original Juniper cover. (See pages 26-7.)

Notice that the amount of the undergrowth in the woodlands varies with the amount of light passing through the tree canopy, the closeness of the trees and the amount of grazing which takes place. Beech trees, especially, with their flat leaves forming a mosiac, cast a deep shade and there is never very much undergrowth underneath them. Below other broad-leaved trees there is often a shrubby undergrowth made up of small trees such as Hawthorn and

Elder and bushes including the native Bramble and alien Laurel, Rhododendron and Snowberry, some of them self-sown. Where the shrubby layer is sparse and the light which gets through the tree canopy can penetrate to the ground, there is usually a rich cover of herbaceous plants — plants which form no woody stems. On the soil surface there may be mosses and lichens, and if very damp, liverworts.

A woodland, with its tiers of vegetation, provides shelter and food for a very wide range of birds, mammals and insects. It is a very complex community with countless food chains intricately linked together in the food webs within it.

Readers may find it interesting to work out food webs for each habitat. Below is an example of a woodland one.

A Woodland Food Web

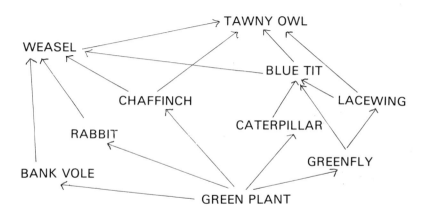

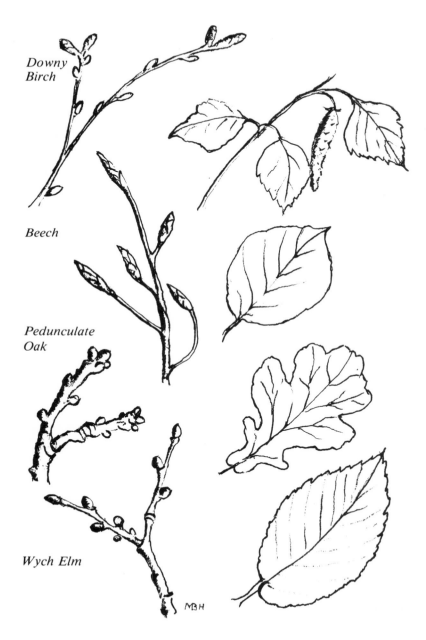

Downy Birch

Beech

Pedunculate Oak

Wych Elm

Figure 8a

Lime

Sycamore

Ash

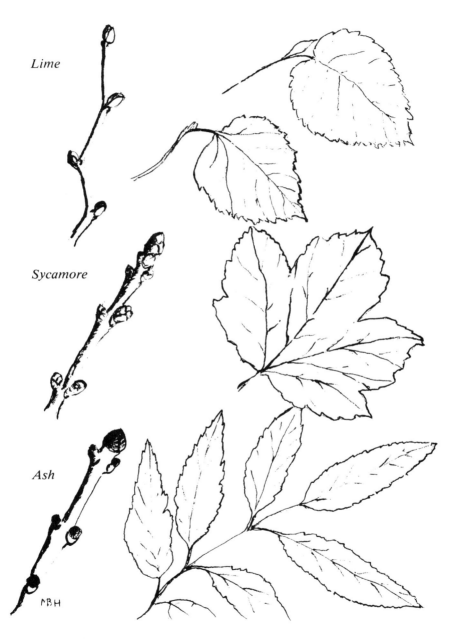

MBH

Figure 8b

Most of the herbaceous plants of a woodland come into leaf and flower before the tree leaves are out; food is built up during the previous season and stored in underground organs to enable them to do this. Typical woodland plants which may be seen in woods passed through on the walks include Dog's Mercury, producing inconspicuous green flowers very early in the season, Common Dog Violet, Primrose, Wood Sorrel, Ramsons and later Herb Robert or Wild Geranium and Wood Avens. After flowering the leaves of some of them do not die down. For example, in Primrose, Dog's Mercury and Violet the leaves go on growing and carrying on photosynthesis in a limited way all through the summer.

Woodland soil is particularly rich in threads or hyphae of fungi, some of which, known as mycorrhiza, are associated with the tree roots. They help the roots absorb water and minerals. Although they cannot be seen without a microscope the fruiting bodies of these fungi are usually much in evidence above the soil surface in the autumn, especially during a wet season.

Grassland

Much of the land which was once covered with trees is now covered with grass, regeneration having been prevented through grazing or cutting for hay. The type of grassland varies with the soil on which it grows.

On the uncultivated hillsides of the Pentlands there is much grassland growing on the acid soil derived from sandstones and shales. The main grasses on this lime-free soil are Common Bent-grass and Wavy Hair-grass, whose tussocky habits produce an uneven surface. Other grasses include Sheep's Fescue and Creeping Soft-grass. Where it is very dry Mat-grass, recognised by its flowers all being on one side of the stem, becomes dominant; where wet, Purple Moor-grass is more abundant. All stages between these two extremes will be seen on the Pentland Walk. Sheep dislike Bracken and Whin and you will see that at many places on the hillside these plants have spread considerably. Low growing plants, such as Heath Bedstraw and Tormentil, are usually present amongst the grasses.

Where soil is derived from rocks containing lime, for example on parts of Arthur's Seat and Craiglockhart Hill, the grassland is quite distinctive from that seen on lime-free soil. Sheep's Fescue, a grass found in short turf on all dry soils whether lime-free or lime-rich is often dominant with lime-loving grasses. e.g. Meadow Oat-grass and Crested Hair-grass amongst it, as well as other lime-loving plants such as Common Rock Rose and Weld (Dyer's Rocket).

In the garden area of the Hermitage Walk (see Walk 2) will be seen grasses which predominate on neutral soil, often planted in

Figure 9a: a *Mat-grass* Nardus stricta
                b *Sheep's Fescue* Festuca ovina
                c *Common Bent-grass* Agrostis tenuis
                d *Crested Hair-grass* Koeleria cristata
                e *Wavy Hair-grass* Deschampsia flexuosa
                f *Purple Moor-grass* Molinia caerulea

Figure 9b: g *Creeping Soft-grass* Holcus mollis
            h *Cock's Foot* Dactylis glomerata
            i *Perennial Rye-grass* Lolium perenne
            j *Timothy* Phleum pratense
            k *Annual Meadow-grass* Poa annua
            l *False Oat-grass* Arrhenatherum elatius

pastures. They include Meadow Fescue, Meadow Foxtail, Perennial Rye-grass and Cock's-foot. Permanent pasture treated with lime to neutralise the acid in the soil will be passed through on the walks in the agricultural areas of Edinburgh. Some of the hill pastures have undergone this treatment after drainage.

Insects and other invertebrates are abundant on grassland.

Upland heath (heather moor)

Grassland of the acid soil gives way to heathland or heather moorland on peaty ground near the summits of the Pentlands. Within the Edinburgh boundary the heather areas are not large and on walks on Caerketton and Allermuir the heather line is crossed and recrossed. Amongst the Heather, Bilberry (Blaeberry) — a deciduous undershrub with pinkish green flowers and purplish black berries, Crowberry — an evergreen heather-like plant in appearance but with a white line down the back of the leaf and with glossy black berries in late summer — and Bell Heather are frequent as well as Bracken and Whin (Gorse). In the wetter parts there is some Cross-leaved Heath.

Heather may be periodically burnt to encourage new plant growth which is tastier for sheep and grouse. Burning also destroys seedlings which have sprung up and so halts the process of succession.

As on grassland invertebrate animals are abundant. Some birds which may be seen on the Pentlands are given in Walk 3. Mammals do not often show up but sometimes a Mountain Hare (introduced into the Pentlands in the middle of the 19th century) may be seen or perhaps a Stoat or Weasel hunting in the grass for mice and voles and taking cover in a nearby stone wall.

Hedgerows and roadside verges

Today there are hedges of Hawthorn around fields and at roadsides on the outskirts of Edinburgh, and within the suburbs many hedges of Privet as well as shrubs, such as Barberry, enclose gardens.

Most of the hedges on the outskirts, which will be passed on the walks, must have been planted as field boundaries after the passing of the Parliamentary Enclosure Acts at the end of the 18th century. Hawthorn was used, as it forms a prickly barrier to farm animals. As the hedges grew up, animal life originally belonging to woodland took up its abode in them. When woodland disappeared they became more and more important as habitats, and as Edinburgh spread many of them came within the Edinburgh Boundary.

Even the suburban Privet hedge provides a home for larvae of some moths such as the Magpie and Small Ermine. The Hawthorn hedge not only supplies the food plant for very many more moth larvae but also forms, with its associated trees and bushes, a corridor for all wildlife connecting together copses and groups of trees. Corridors of bushes and trees connect the suburbs of Edinburgh with the Pentland Hills.

Not surprisingly herbaceous plants which grow in association with hedges are those likely to be encountered in the lighter part of a broad-leaved wood, for example: Common Dog Violet, Herb Robert and Wood Avens. Climbing plants, such as Honeysuckle and Cleavers, often called Sticky Willie, are often present for they have some means of scrambling upwards to the light. Along the length of parts of a hedge there is often a zone of Umbellifers, e.g. Cow Parsley (see Walk 5), which provides a habitat for insects of all shapes and sizes.

Associated with hedges are road verges covered with grassland. The latter may not have been disturbed by ploughing for years and consequently often support a rich flora of herbaceous plants. There is a verge on the outskirts of Balerno, now within the Edinburgh Boundary, of about 100 yards (91 m) in length on which over 50 flowering plants have been recorded, including Crosswort, Lesser Stitchwort, Meadow Vetchling and Astrantia.

The herbaceous plants growing on a verge vary not only with the age of the grassland and type of soil on which the grass is growing but also with the amount and time of verge cutting which takes place and whether or not it has been sprayed with herbicide. At the edge of busy roads the plants must be tough to be able to resist fumes from car exhausts and, in winter, salt spray used as a de-icer. The grass verge is a very valuable habitat for butterfly larvae.

Fresh water habitats

Fresh water habitats for wildlife are becoming rarer today as more and more drainage takes place. Edinburgh is fortunate that it includes within its boundary part of the Water of Leith in which water flows for only 23 miles (37 km) — many of these within the City Boundary — from the Pentlands to the Firth of Forth, providing at one time water power for mills along its way; the Braid Burn and Niddrie Burn, the Union Canal with its long stretch of slowly moving water, reservoirs and lakes, e.g. Duddingston Loch and some smaller watery expanses or ponds, such as Figgate and Lochend Park Ponds full of stationary water.

In all the water habitats the vegetation is zoned unless the edge is stone-faced. Walking along the bank of a waterway or the side of a lake or pond you will see an open water zone bordered by a swamp zone of shallow water merging into a marsh zone of water-logged soil. There follows a diagram of the cross section of a pond:

In the open water zone, where the water is not moving rapidly and is not too deep, there may be plants rooted to the bottom, some with

MARSH   SWAMP   OPEN WATER

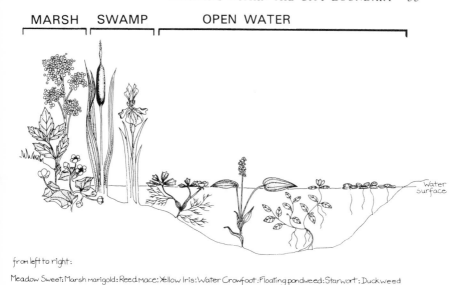

from left to right:

Meadow Sweet: Marsh marigold: Reed mace: Yellow Iris: Water Crowfoot: Floating pondweed: Starwort: Duckweed

Figure 10:   Cross section of a pond

floating leaves and flowers raised in the air, e.g Floating Pondweed, Water Crowfoot, Amphibious Bistort, Fringed Water-lily, others totally submerged, e.g. Canadian Pondweed, Water Starwort. Other plants in still water or slowly moving water are free floating either on the surface of the water, e.g. Duckweed, or underneath the surface. The latter group includes the green algae — lowly non-flowering plants which often turn the water into a kind of green soup.

Included in the list of plants growing in the swamp zone are Yellow Iris, Bog Bean, Bur-reed, Reed-mace, all seen at Duddingston Loch where the Common Reed covers several acres at the west and southern end,

whilst amongst the plants seen in the marsh zone are Marsh Marigold, Ragged Robin, Marsh Horsetail and Meadowsweet, which also abounds in large patches along the side of the Canal.

The animal life of a fresh water habitat is very varied and prolific. In summer insects, such as Dragonfly, Damselfly, Mayfly, Caddis Fly species and Gnat, and birds, such as the Swift, Swallow and House Martin, fly over the water. Birds which may be seen on the open water and inhabiting the vegetation around the edge of Duddingston Loch — a Bird Sanctuary — are given in the appendix, those which may be seen at Blackford Pond are described in Walk 2. Mammals seen in the marsh zone of the Water of Leith, for example, include Water Vole, sometimes incorrectly named Water Rat, which is abundant, and escaped Mink.

To appreciate fully the great richness of animal life in unpolluted water it is necessary to spend time with a net 'dipping' from the bank or looking on the under surface of stones taken from the water. A list of animals seen during a short evening 'dip' in the Braid Burn is given on page 59. It is, however, possible to see a number of water animals just by 'looking'.

Look for animals on the surface film — the boundary between air and water. You may, for example, see a Pond Skater, with its long slender legs spreading its light weight over a large area, moving jerkily over the surface of the water. Under the film and hanging on to it you may sometimes see a species of Pond Snail and the larvae and pupae of Mosquito.

Freely swimming in the water can be seen water insects such as the plant sap-sucking Water Boatman (*Corixa*), the predatory Water Bug *Notonecta* swimming on its back; fish, such as Three-spined Stickleback found in most water masses, Pike, common in Duddingston Loch, Trout seen in the Braid Burn and even the Salmon on the Almond, where there is a fish ladder. Amphibia (Frogs, Toads and Newts) occur in some Edinburgh ponds and larger water masses — see the booklet *Ponds in the Lothians* produced by the Lothians Branch of the Scottish Wildlife Trust.

When water habitats are untouched by man gradual development takes place to the climax community. Thus if the canal were not managed open water would change in the first place into swamp and marsh, and the bank verge into scrub and woodland. This is not allowed to happen, for dredging and cutting halt in the succession. Ponds, lochs and the Canal have to be cleared from time to time but on the edge of the Water of Leith the movement of the water prevents any silting and makes clearing unnecessary.

Bogs

Bogs are very wet areas with acid peat on which Sphagnum moss grows. Like other watery habitats they have decreased in number over the year through drainage. When, however, the City expanded in 1975 a very fine bog, the Red Moss or Balerno Common, at the foot of the Pentlands came within the City Boundary. It is now a Nature Reserve under the management of the Scottish Wildlife Trust.

This bogland became built up after the Ice Age. When the ice receded over 5000 years ago the Balerno area became covered with a boulder clay sheet and the present Moss area must have been a shallow hollow in this. After water collected Sphagnum mosses and Cotton Grass came in. As the Sphagnum died down under its growing surface, acid peat built up in the water-logged conditions which favour its formation. The vegetational history of the Moss has been worked out by removing cores of peat and examining fossil pollen grains found in the different levels under the microscopic (see page 17).

If you look towards the Moss from the surrounding road you will see that the area is dome-shaped, the peat having built up more quickly on the central parts where drainage is least effective. After that walk to the edge of the bog surface — visitors are asked not to go onto the bog surface as it is very fragile and not safe — and from there you will see a mosaic of boggy hollows filled chiefly with Sphagnum and raised hummocks on which grow Cotton-grass and Heather. As on a Heather moor the Heather is accompanied by Bilberry (Blaeberry), Crowberry, Bell Heather and on the wetter edges of the hummocks, Cross-leaved Heath.

Coastal water habitats

Edinburgh has 15 miles (24 km) of coastline. Much of it is built up with docks and other works and the five miles of wooded shore, added to the west of the District in 1975, are not easily accessible to the public. A sandy shore merges into one of soft mud at Cramond where the River Almond enters the Firth. This area is included in one of the walks. A visit to Cramond Island provides an opportunity to examine a rocky shore habitat.

Sandy and muddy shore

A stretch of shore which is exposed after the tide goes out appears, at first, to be without much life, but soon evidence of sand-dwelling animals may be made out. Casts and holes made by the Lugworm will probably be seen, also sandy tubes of the Sand-mason worm and where it is muddy, fine tubes of Peacock worm sticking three to four inches (7-10 cm) out of the ground. Empty shells of many shellfish such as the Common Cockle, distinguished by its globular ridged shell, Razor Shells, so-called because of their resemblance to a cut-throat razor, will be seen washed up here as well as in the sand above high tide. Their owners when alive live in the sand between the tide lines or below the low-tide mark. Shellfish are related to land snails belonging to the group of animals known as Molluscs.

The shore animals are very active when the tide is in and can survive when the tide goes out. They adapt themselves to their environment in various ways. They must be able to burrow in order to resist the incoming water and to prevent drying out when the tide goes out. They must be able to get food. How they do this illustrates several ways in which animals may become adapted to a shore environment. Some examples of animals found on the Cramond beach which illustrate different feeding methods are now given.

The Lugworm which is responsible for the worm casts is

about eight inches (20 cm) long. It does not form a tube, but lives always under the sand strengthening the walls of its U-shaped burrows with mucus (see Figure 11a). It obtains its food in a way similar to the Landworm, swallowing great quantities of sand. In the sand there is organic debris which the animal digests and absorbs, while the undigested sand passes out as casts. The Lugworm is commonest where there is a good admixture of organic matter in the sand.

Unlike the Lugworm the Peacock worm, commonly seen at Cramond, forms a tube from which it puts brightly coloured tentacles when the tide is in. The tentacles are covered with little hairs which collect food suspended in the water. At low tide the tentacles are withdrawn within the tube.

Many of the shellfish, including Cockle and Razor shell, burrow in the sand and sieve particles of food from the water. These are examples of bivalves which are shellfish with laterally compressed bodies enclosed by a two-valved hinged shell. The valves are united by elastic ligaments. When the valves open the animal, still suspended in sand, draws in a continuous stream of water through a siphon at its hind end (see Figure 11b). As in the Peacock worm suspended matter is filtered out of the water.

Thin Tellin with the familiar rose-pink delicate shell which flattens out to give the appearance of butterfly wings, often found on Cramond beach, is an example of a shellfish feeding in yet another way. The animal is buried in the sand but when the tide is in it extends a feeding siphon like a

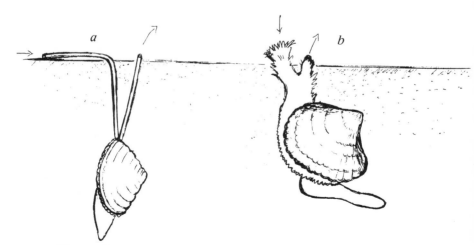

Figure 11: *Diagrammatic sketches of some seashore animals*
  a *Thin Tellin* Tellina tenuis (*a deposit feeder*)
  b *Common Cockle* Cardium edule (*a suspension feeder*)

Figure 11:   c *Acorn Barnacle* Batanus Calanoides
d *Lugworm* Arenicola marina

miniature vacuum cleaner to grope for food on top of the sand and to take in bits of organic matter (see Figure 11d). The siphon is the part of the animal which is eaten by sand fish such as sand eels and flatfish. When this happens the siphon grows again and the shellfish is not harmed. In muddier places empty shells of Macoma, a close relative of Thin Tellin, are found.

Readers may wonder how these animals get their position in the sand in the first place. The young bivalves are free living in the water, but eventually they settle down in the sand. Larval Lugworms, on the other hand, spend their early days on the bottom and burrow directly into the sand.

Empty shells of Univalves — marine snails in which the shell is in one piece and usually spiral — are found amongst the bivalve shells. As there is no surface for attachment on the sand for the living animals the shells must have washed off rocks, barrier walls or breakwaters or from barnacles which give them footing.

Mussels are bivalves which are attached to stones or rocks by horny threads acting like guy ropes and on the gravelly part of the shore, as at Cramond, they may be collected together to form a mussel bed. Although not buried in the sand they are filter feeders like the Cockle. They are often covered with Barnacles and freely moving Periwinkles, two animals typical of a rocky shore (see above).

The Mussel may be a public health risk as it is one animal which thrives in a moderate degree of sewage pollution. At Cramond a notice warns the public not to collect them for eating.

On the shore-line wading birds

can be seen probing in the sand or mud for small molluscs or crustaceans. Many, such as the Turnstone, are winter visitors. The black and white Oyster-catcher, recognised by its pink legs and long orange beak, is a specialist at probing for Cockles and other bivalves, which it prises open.

Rocky shore

The animals found typically on a rocky shore are those which must have some means of attachment. Some may be seen on the Cramond Walk on the barrier wall or attached to the larger stones. They may be observed more easily, along with the different coloured seaweeds on Cramond Island, and on the side of the causeway leading to it.
(*Note*: If you plan to walk along the causeway to Cramond Island be sure to check the times of High Water; it is very easy to get marooned there.)

All seaweeds, a group of non-flowering plants, contain chlorophyll although it may be masked by brown or red pigments. Like green plants living on the land they are able to carry out photosynthesis, building up food on which the sea animals depend. Green seaweeds, such as Sea Ribbon with its tubular fronds, Sea Lettuce with bright green fronds like a wavy lettuce leaf, are found nearest high water mark and build up food most effectively in bright light; red seaweeds, such as Plumularia, with its feather-like dingy red coloured branches

hanging in tufts, which are at the lowest levels and in rock pools, usually under water even at low tide, are capable of carrying on photosynthesis even in a dull light, while brown seaweeds which grow in the zone between the green and red ones are intermediate in their light requirements. Examples of brown seaweeds found at Cramond are Bladder Wrack, with a repeatedly forked thallus (the word used for the body of the seaweed) and paired bladders which buoy it up; Flat or Spiral Wrack found at a slightly higher level than the Bladder Wrack. It has no air bladders but can be recognised by the twisted ends of the side branches.

Seaside flowering plants found on Cramond Island include Sea Campion, Buck's-horn Plantain and Thrift or Sea Pink which forms a carpet of pink-coloured blossom in early summer on the rocky shore.

The commonest animals on the rocks are Barnacle, Limpet and Periwinkle (more than one species). Although the Barnacle (see Figure 11c) looks like a shellfish it is a member of the crab family which has taken up a sedentary existence. With its appendages which correspond to the legs of a crab it combs the water for small animals and plants on which it feeds. The Limpet, which is difficult to dislodge from a rock when the tide is out, moves about when the tide is in, rasping vegetable food off the rock by means of its horny tongue covered with teeth. It returns, when the tide goes out, to the exact spot which it left. The Periwinkle or Sea Snail also feeds on vegetation but it moves about even when exposed to the atmosphere. Like the land snail it has an air cavity which it uses as a kind of lung closing the outside opening when the tide comes in.

Built-up areas

Much natural history may be studied within built-up areas.

The inside of buildings provides a clearly defined habitat harbouring a large selection of animals including Spider, insects such as Clothes Moth and in dampish places Silverfish, as well as the occasional mammal such as the House Mouse in private houses and the Black Rat and Brown Rat at the docks and warehouses.

Outside, the ledges and crevices of buildings develop a community of their own providing shelter and breeding places for birds, such as House Sparrow, Feral Pigeon — a descendent of the Rock Dove which is at home on wild cliffs — Starling and Collared Dove which only arrived in Edinburgh in the early 1960s. A pair of Kestrels has been known to nest on office buildings near the east end of Princes Street and in the Edinburgh Natural History Journal of 1881-2 there is an account of the roosting of the Peregrine Falcon on the spires of St Mary's Cathedral.

The summer visiting Swift and House Martin may be seen flying around buildings in the City centre, the Swift nesting in crannies high up on buildings and the House Martin fixing its mud nest under the eaves of houses.

Not all Starlings stay to roost in the City centre, but towards evening may collect together and fly to some communal roost on the outskirts. There is a huge roost consisting of thousands on the Forth Road Bridge.

Although the City parks and gardens vary a great deal in size, amount of ground cover and the extent to which they are cultivated, much vegetation within them, like the hedgerows, can be thought of as a slice of woodland edge. They harbour resident birds such as Blackbird, Song Thrush, Blue Tit, Great Tit, Dunnock, Robin, Carrion Crow and Magpie and even the occasional Chaffinch and Greenfinch. Visiting birds will be mentioned on walks. The Royal Botanic Garden with its rich collection of trees and shrubs is a haven for all kinds of birds, some otherwise usually only seen outside the City Boundary.

Mammals are no strangers to the City. Bats are seen on summer evenings in most of the public parks, while Roe Deer have been sighted on several occasions on Craiglockhart Hill; Rabbits are abundant in Holyrood Park and will be seen on Corstorphine Hill and at Blackford. Hedgehogs have been seen in gardens as has the occasional Brown Hare. Grey and Common Seals occur beyond the Sea Wall at Leith Docks, especially on the nearby rocks.

Badgers moved up to the outskirts of the City at the end of last century, so with the explosion of growth of the City their setts are now well within the boundary. Foxes, too, have adapted to City life, and have been known to breed in the Royal Botanic Garden. Grey Squirrels are common throughout the area and may be seen on any of the walks.

Walls form an interesting micro-habitat in a built-up area, providing an initial footing place for non-flowering plants — algae, lichens, mosses, and ferns. Two mosses usually present on old walls everywhere are the Wall Screw Moss and the Grey Cushion Moss.

As many non-flowering plants are particularly sensitive to pollution, the number of species found increases as one passes to the outskirts. Notice that many more are to be seen on old walls and trees on the Cramond Walk than on any walls or tree trunks seen on a walk through a City park.

Sea birds on the edge of the estuary in the dockland area

Within the built-up area valuable vantage points from which to view sea birds of open water and mud flats are Leith Docks and Seafield foreshore to the east. Both can be reached by bus or car. The Docks are open to the public, walking or in cars, except Newhaven Breakwater and East Breakwater which are out of bounds.

A good acreage of Leith Docks was reclaimed from the Firth of Forth by tipping. Some of the tipped material became washed away and spread out to form a mud flat between the Sea Wall and nearby rocks (Middle Craig Rocks). Almost every bird on the two lists in the appendix has been recorded here. Before the land was built on for oil related activities it attracted many birds, including Green Sandpiper, Shore Lark and Snow Bunting. One great feature on the Docks is the Stone Island formed when a new entrance was cut to the Imperial Dock. It became a ternery and being completely isolated is quite safe. Up to 70 pairs of Common Tern have bred there. If the surface were improved by addition of gravel and/or turf it could be even better.

Where the Seafield foreshore begins there is a sewage outfall. Here masses of gulls congregate scavenging for food. This part of the Firth of Forth is of international status as a wintering area for Scaup and Pochard. The shore has for many years attracted a large winter flock of Greenfinch that feed upon the insect life in the rotting seaweed.

You may not get a Slavonian Grebe (seen Edinburgh Dock 10 June 1966) or a Little Auk (seen December-January 1955-56) or a Storm Petrel (seen 30 November 1965) but you should enjoy a visit to both Leith Docks and Seafield foreshore.

Wasteland

In the centre of the cities as well as in the suburbs and on the outskirts there are some areas of relatively undisturbed wasteland, land which has been used by Man but at the current time not being cared for. It may be a vacant building plot or a site scheduled for redevelopment in some way or other. The soil probably is lime-rich containing calcium carbonate from cement rubble.

At first the land is bare and if it remains undisturbed for long enough it is often possible to follow the stages in its colonisation or succession to the time when it is covered with vegetation, eventually becoming scrubby supporting seedlings of bushes, for example those of Elder, Bramble and the garden escape, Buddleia or Butterfly plant, well-named as it is so attractive to butterflies.

Some examples of waste ground in various stages of colonisation will be passed by on the course of walks, others will no doubt be noticed when wandering through Edinburgh, for example, the open ground of the old Currie goods yard, the unmade-up car parks of the Lothian Road opposite the Usher Hall, wasteland of the Dock area, wasteland adjacent to Warriston Cemetery.

The first plants to become established include those such as Groundsel, Shepherd's Purse, Hairy Bittercress — readers with gardens will be only too familiar with these rapidly appearing garden weeds — which have effective seed dispersal and grow very quickly, having several life cycles in one year (that is, producing several lots of seeds).

Other plants which arrive as a result of effective wind dispersal include Rosebay Willowherb — once established the Willowherb spreads rapidly by vigorous growth — Colts-foot and species of Thistles. One

of the most widespread thistles of waste places is Spear Thistle. Some of the perennials of waste ground, e.g. Couch Grass, Celandine, may have regenerated readily from fragments of root or underground stem, which have been in the ground for some time.

Among the colonisers there may be aliens which have come in from abroad by some means or other. A common one, usually in wasteland around farms and on tracks and paths in the Edinburgh District, is Pineappleweed, a native of Asia. It is thought that its fruits have spread from ports of entry on the wheels of motor cars. Another alien which reached the Edinburgh area in the 1950s and is now widespread, is Oxford Ragwort, a native of Sicily, cultivated in the Oxford Botanical Garden for over 200 years and escaping from it in the 19th century. Probably it spread along railway tracks in the vortex of air following trains. As it is an annual and has no means of spreading vegetatively it tends to become crowded out when the waste ground becomes colonised by other plants.

Growing on the wasteland of the Dock areas, now diminishing as new buildings grow up, there is usually a rich collection of casual plants, which vary from year to year. In 1976 and 1977, for example, they included Thorn-apple, Tree Lupin, Ragweed (all three from abroad), the cultivated Flax and Wild Radish (doubtfully native). Plants which are usually plentiful every year on this wasteland include Ribbed (Yellow) Melilot, Small Melilot, Eastern Rocket, three plants introduced into Britain and now well-established, and the native Mugwort and Wormwood.

Giant Hogweed, a garden escape which was popular in gardens in Victorian times, grows on some railway sidings and other pieces of waste ground including that beneath the Castle. It may reach ten feet (three m) high or more. It should not be handled, except when wearing thick gloves, as in sunlight the volatile substance it contains may produce blisters on the skin.

Another distinctive garden escape now found beside the Water of Leith is the strong scented Indian or Himalayan Balsam, also known as the Policeman's Helmet because of its hooded purplish flowers.

Some Walks through Edinburgh's Countryside

Walk 1: Through Holyrood Park

Towering 823 feet (251 m) above the River Forth, the craggy hill known as Arthur's Seat dominates the City of Edinburgh with a majestic outline resembling that of a crouching lion. At the base of the hill sits the Royal Residence of Holyrood House. Arthur's Seat and the surrounding parkland comprises the Crown Property of Holyrood Park.

Holyrood Park is an area of undoubted historical and scientific interest. The lands of the Park at one time formed the ancient Sanctuary of Holyrood to which persons in financial difficulty could gain safety from their creditors for a period of twenty-four hours. The Park's beauty has inspired many literary works. Much of Sir Walter Scott's famous novel, *Heart of Midlothian*, is set within its confines. Early Man's association with the Park is evidenced by ancient cultivation terraces and hut circles and much of Scotland's history is enshrined in the adjacent Holyrood Palace and Abbey. Holyrood Park is, however, most famous for its geological interest and has since the 18th century been a mecca for geologists world wide.

Vegetation The vegetation of Holyrood is rough grassland with areas of shrubs, particularly Whin (Gorse) which grows widely on all hill slopes. Other shrubs seen are Bramble, Wild Rose, Blackthorn and low shrubby trees of Sycamore, Sessile Oak and Whitebeam. There is no natural woodland left, but trees grow around the margins and there is a little deciduous woodland in parts of Duddingston Bird Sanctuary.

Much of the grassland vegetation is composed of grasses typical of acid soil with accompanying herbaceous plants. In June and July when you walk up the Long Row notice that the grassland on either side of the path is dominated by Sheep's Meadow Fescue and Red Fescue, while on the walk up the Lion's Head the dominant grasses are Common Bent, Wavy Hair-grass with some Fescues. Amongst the grasses are herbaceous plants, typical of grassy heathland, such as Heath Bedstraw, Tormentil and Sheep's Sorrel.

In contrast, the soil of the Radical Road is derived from non-acidic rocks. In summer look on the grassland on either side of the path and you will see lime-loving grasses such as Meadow Oat-grass and Crested Hair-grass, as well as the lime-loving Common Rock-rose, Weld and Viper's Bugloss. At the bottom of the cliff where the soil is more acid there is much Wood Sage.

Over 200 flowering plants, several of them relatively rare, grow in the Park. Common ones which may be seen on the circular walk are listed in the appendix.

Mammals   Some of the shrub-covered slopes support numerous rabbits, causing considerable erosion of the soil. Judging from the varied colours of the rabbit population, many must be descendants of tame pet rabbits which have been released in the Park.

The extensive rough grassland provides a suitable environment for voles and shrews which are hunted by kestrels, foxes and the occasional weasel.

Mink have been known to visit Duddingston Loch.

Starting point   This circular walk begins at Holyrood Car Park which may be reached by private car or bus, Nos. 6, 45, 60.

Distance   3 miles (4.8 km). Allow plenty of time as most of the way is hill walking.

Visitors are strongly advised to wear stout footwear and carry a light waterproof. The use of geological hammers anywhere in the Park is forbidden by law as is the picking of wild flowers. The Park is patrolled by a uniformed constabulary who are usually most willing to help or advise visitors.

It is expected that visitors will need to refer to the map frequently in order to follow the route described.

Pause for a few minutes in the car park. You are now standing on the site of *Holyrood Loch*, one of Edinburgh's post-glacial lochs. The loch, centred on Holyrood House, covered a triangular area with a base line stretching from the Salisbury Crags over to the houses behind Holyrood House. The existence of Holyrood Loch is based mainly on geological evidence though some reference was made to a lake or piece of marshy ground at the foot of Arthur's Seat in an old description of Holyrood. In any case, the ancient

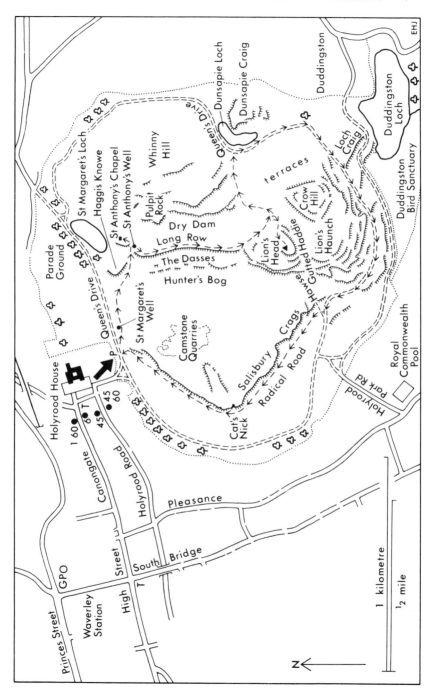

loch must have dried up long before Holyrood Abbey was founded at the beginning of the 12th century as King David, the 'sair Sanct', was not likely to choose a soft morass on which to erect such an important building. The loch is thought to have been between 30 to 40 feet (9-12 m) deep in places. Eventually, like most lochs of this type, it became silted up with material brought down by streams which flowed into it. One of those streams is thought to have flowed along the base of the Salisbury Crags while another flowed in from the west carrying drainage from the Nor' Loch. Eventually, as the loch dried out it became a peat bog full of twigs of birch, hazel and other trees which no doubt at one time formed part of the ancient Forest of Drumsheugh which grew in the vicinity.

Now walk towards the Haggis Knowe (see map). About 75 yards (69 m) beyond the car park observe the ornamental well built into the hillside. This is *St Margaret's Well*, which was rebuilt on this site in 1862, having been removed from its original location at nearby Restalrig Village where it had been threatened by the construction of the North British Railway Yards. One of the attractive features of the well is its miniature Gothic style arches. The well is supplied by a fresh water spring which is reputed to stay cool even at the height of summer.

About 150 yards (137 m) beyond St Margaret's Well stands the low west-facing cliff known as the *Haggis Knowe* or *Cockleshell*.

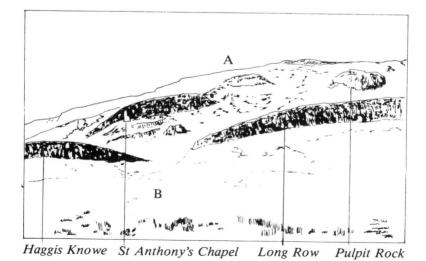

Haggis Knowe   St Anthony's Chapel   Long Row   Pulpit Rock
                                                    Vent

Figure 12:   A line between A and B marks the approximate line of St Anthony's Fault

Make your way over to the path which runs through the hollow separating the Haggis Knowe from the Long Row, an ascending cliff-crowned ridge. This hollow represents the eroded line of a minor fault, known as the *St Anthony's Fault* which continues up behind the ruin of St Anthony's chapel and over Whinny Hill (see map). At one time the Haggis Knowe was a northward continuation of the Long Row but due to the action of the fault the Haggis Knowe has been offset some distance to the west in relation to the Long Row. The Long Row represents *Lava I* which was erupted from the Castle Rock Vent.

Look ahead of you at the ruin of *St Anthony's Chapel*, sitting sentinel-like on a rocky promontory. The foundations of the chapel are built directly on *Lava III* which was erupted from the Pulpit Rock Vent located on the west slope of Whinny Hill. This lava is easily recognised by its columnar structure. The upper part of the flow forms the cliff above and to the east of the chapel.

As you climb up the path towards the chapel, you pass a large smooth boulder, known as an erratic — a loose rock different from its neighbours left over from the Ice Age — which marks the site of *St Anthony's Well*. Although now sealed off for health reasons, it is interesting to note that this well, really a fresh water spring, received its water supply from ground water accumulated in the shatter belt of St Anthony's Fault. The well is referred to in an old Scottish song:

Now Arthur's Seat shall be my bed,
The sheets shall never be pressed by me;
St Anton's Well shall be my drink,
Since my true love's forsaken Me!

Before falling into its present ruinous condition, St Anthony's Chapel was described as a beautiful Gothic building. It was 43 feet (13 m) long, 18 feet (5.5 m) broad and 18 feet (5.5 m) high with a square tower of sides 19 feet (6 m) at its west end. The Hermitage and Chapel of St Anthony is believed to have formed a dependency of the Preceptory at Leith and to have been placed there to catch the eye of seamen as they entered or departed from the Forth, when their offering and vows would be made to the patron saint and the hermit who ministered at the altar.

From the doorway of the Chapel, look over St Margaret's Loch to the area laid out as a playing field. The flat area is known as the Parade Ground. Here in August 1881 the military spectacle which came to be described as the 'Wet Review' took place. Her Majesty Queen Victoria, before a vast number of spectators, reviewed a force of 40,000 Scottish Volunteers. So many men under arms had not been massed together in Scotland since James IV marched to Flodden. The colourful spectacle was unfortunately marred by a continuous downpour of rain. Hence the description – 'Wet Review'.

From the St Anthony's chapel promontory runs the Long Row, the cliff-crowned ridge which extends southwards for half a mile (0.8 km) up to the base of the Lion's Head. The line of the St Anthony's Fault can also be clearly seen from this vantage point. The eastern slope of the Long Row is separated from the high ground of Whinny Hill (see map) to the east, by a valley known as the Dry Dam. Following the map carefully, descend from St Anthony's Chapel and over the northern end of the Dry Dam ascend the eastern slopes of the Long Row to the footpath which runs parallel to the edge of the cliff. Look across the Dry Dam and a large boss of rock will be seen on the slope opposite. This is the *Pulpit Rock Vent*, the small lava-filled parasitic vent (see Figure 1) from which *Lava III* was erupted. An interesting feature is the well-developed columnar joining of the basalt formed by the lava which blocked the vent, cooling in the feeder pipe.

Look in the opposite direction to the west and you will see the broad valley known as *Hunter's Bog*. This was at one stage occupied by a shallow glacial loch.

Continue up the Long Row for about 200 yards (183 m) and look westward again over Hunter's Bog. On the distant slope you will see a series of spoil heaps from workings now no longer used, known as the *Camstone Quarries*. The quarries are so named because one of the rocks quarried there was used in the past by proud Edinburgh housewives to scour their front doorsteps. The scouring stone was known as Camstone.

Look below you (west) and you will see a line of low west-facing cliffs known as the *Dasses*. Although apparently similar in form to the Long Row, the Dasses are not lava flows but a set of intrusive basalt sills. On the flat shelf above the Dasses were discovered a group of six stone hut circles. These primitive prehistoric dwellings provide evidence of early Man's occupation of the area. The Dasses would provide a safe and secure site for a settlement overlooking the post-glacial lake. The small spring on the shelf would also have provided a convenient source of fresh water.

Continue up the ridge until you reach a small gully. The gully marks the point at which the *Lion's Head Vent* breached the Long Row to erupt *Lava II*. After the eruption, the vent slowly filled with rock debris forming agglomerate. The second and last eruption from the Lion's Head Vent was *Lava IV* which was intruded through the agglomerate. When this eruption ceased, the residue of the lava remaining in the vent, cooled, and blocked the Lion's Head Vent for the last time.

Figure 13: *The Long Row looking from Haggis Knowe to the*
Lion's Head Summit, showing where it has been
breached by the vent.

Cross the gully and follow the footpath to the summit. On a clear
day the Lion's Head provides an excellent viewpoint from which
many of the important features of the landscape can be observed.

Use the direction indicator on the summit as a guide. To the north lies the Firth of Forth with the island of Inchkeith in the foreground. Beyond the Forth lies the 'Kingdom of Fife' with intrusive sills forming the Lomond Hills. Following a clockwise direction and a little more to the east, the low white cliff (a sill) of the May Island sits far out in the Forth. Continuing the traverse, you will see some of the intrusive rocks of East Lothian, the Bass Rock and North Berwick Law, both volcanic plugs, and the Traprain Law lacolith (see Map 1). To the south-east can be seen the long line of the Lammermuir and Moorfoot Hills and to the south the prominent ridge of the Pentland Hills. Still to the south but lying at a lower level are Blackford Hill (see Walk 2) and the Braid Hills, which are composed of volcanic rocks. To the west lies the West Lothian Oil Shale fields, the first oil industry in the world, with their prominent red waste bings standing as a monument to this once famous industry. Finally, if the day is really clear, you may be rewarded wih a glimpse of the Scottish Highlands to the north-west.

From the viewpoint note the summit of Crow Hill below you to the south-east. Crow Hill marks the summit of the Lion's Haunch Vent. It is a mass of basalt capping the agglomerate which filled the vent after the eruption of *Lavas V-XIII*.

To the north-east note the extensive area of broken ground of Whinny Hill, already identified earlier in the walk. It represents the best preserved fragment of the cone and is composed of individual lava flows (*V-XIII*) which erupted from the Lion's Head Vent. It has intercalations of ash.

Figure 14:   Duddingston Loch with the Loch Craig (Lava I) in the foreground

Descend to *Dunsappie Loch*. This loch was formed from an artificially dammed crescent-shaped hollow which had been gouged out by the passage of ice. The loch is dominated by Dunsappie Craig which is a basalt intrusion into the margin of the Lion's Haunch Vent. The loch itself is interesting in that it provides a habitat for a variety of water birds.

Before leaving the loch look up on to the slopes of the Lion's Haunch. If the sun is in the right direction (west) you will see a series of prehistoric cultivation terraces cut into the hillsides.

Continue for about 100 yards (91 m) beyond the south end of Dunsappie Loch and pause at the railing which runs parallel to the Queen's Drive (see map). From this spot you will obtain a fine view of Duddingston Loch and Duddingston village nestling in the hillside below you. As mentioned in the Introduction, there is evidence that prehistoric Man existed in the area. Duddingston Loch, which lies in a shallow basin eroded in soft rocks gouged out by the passage of ice, is now a bird sanctuary. A list of birds living and breeding in the area is given in the appendix. A set of stone steps leads down to Duddingston from the south end of Dunsappie Loch.

Follow the Queen's Drive for another 250 yards (229 m) and below you where the low road leaves the side of Duddingston Loch, observe the south-westerly facing ridge rising steeply from the roadside. This represents another outcrop of *Lava I*; the other was visible in the Long Row, earlier in the walk. There is little doubt that the Loch Craig and the Long Row were originally parts of the same flow; the portion of the flow which once united the two outcrops has been shattered and removed by the positioning of the Lion's Head and Haunch Vents.

To the west of Duddingston Loch is Prestonfield House, surrounded by trees attractively planted in the shape of the ace of clubs. Close by to the west, the golf course displays ridges formed by rigs of old common fields.

Continue along Queen's Drive and look for exposures of vent agglomerate. These will be seen forming parts of the cliffs to the north side of the road. The bright red matrix contains blocks of basalt and sedimentary rocks.

Walk on along the Queen's Drive to a point about 100 yards (91 m) beyond the start of the retaining wall on the north side of the road. Where the road passes through a cutting, a large rock protrudes through the retaining wall at road level. Note the polished appearance of its surface and the near vertical grooves. These grooves and polished surfaces, known as *Slickensides*, were formed as a result of movement of an adjacent rock on a fault plane. The direction of the grooving indicates the direction of the fault movement.

A few yards west, on the same side of the road, also at road level, you will see another protruding rock. It bears horizontal scratches, known as *Glacial Striae*, which were inscribed by the movement of ice as it passed from west to east. You may find it interesting to compare the two surfaces.

Pass through the road cutting where you will no doubt be attracted by the view over old Edinburgh and the Castle and certainly more so by the exciting escarpment known as the *Salisbury Crags*. Make your way to the narrow gap known as the *Hawes* where a footpath cuts through the end of the Salisbury Crags.

From the Hawes look north and you will obtain a fine view of the Hunter's Bog. To the right the steep grassy slopes mark the continuation of the Lion's Head and Haunch Vent Margins. Towering above you is the basalt capped summit of the Lion's Head. The great vertical scar which divides the slopes is known as the Gutted Haddie. This erosion gully was initiated by a cloudburst in the 18th century and has continued to increase in size despite conservation work by the Park Authorities. It is interesting to note that the line of the Gutted Haddie approximates to the vertical junction between the Lion's Head and Haunch Vents.

The west slope of the Hunter's Bog contrasts sharply with that of the east, being an excellent example of a *Dip Slope* associated with the Salisbury Crag Sill which is the next stage of the excursion.

Radical Road and Salisbury Crags   The Salisbury Crags form a prominent west facing semi-circular escarpment running from the base of the Lion's Haunch for a mile (0.8 km) to Holyrood House. It is probably the finest example in Scotland of an igneous sill, that is a sheet of igneous rock intruded in a molten state along the horizontal or near horizontal bedding planes of earlier rocks. In the case of Salisbury Crags, the intrusive rock is a form of dolerite (an igneous rock coarser in grain than basalt) known as teschenite which has been injected into the sandstones. A footpath known as the Radical Road follows the base of the sill throughout its length and provides easy access to all localities of interest.

The Radical Road was constructed in 1820 on the advice of Sir Walter Scott who thought that the work on it would prevent the unemployed from becoming incited by Radical propaganda to some kind of action against the established order.

Hutton's Section   Walk along the Radical Road for about 25 yards (23 m) and turn into the small quarry on your right. This is probably the most famous geological locality on Arthur's Seat and is known as *Hutton's Section*. Here the arrangement of the rocks was used by Scottish geologist James Hutton (1726-1797), one of the founders of modern geology and author of the *Theory of the Earth*, to support his theory regarding the origin of igneous rocks. For details see *The Geology of the Lothians and South East Scotland*.

Return to the Radical Road and continue uphill for about 300 yards (274 m) where you will arrive at the north-west corner of a large quarry. At this corner you will see an eight foot (2.4 m) high rock standing at the edge of the path. Known as *Hutton's Rock* it consists of a conical mass of teschenite with a four-inch (100 mm) band of mineral haematite, an iron ore, running through it. Tradition has it that the quarrymen preserved the rock at Hutton's request.

Continue along the Radical Road and you will see various exposures between the underlying sandstones and the sill. Look out for sandstone which has been crumpled and distorted by its contact with the sill.

Walk on for about 50 yards (46 m) and where the Radical Road begins to dip downhill, you will arrive at a locality known as the *Cat's Nick* (see map). At this locality you will be able to study a fault and a dyke. The *Cat's Nick Fault*, a steep walled cleft, can be recognised as a vertical belt of bleached and decomposed rock about 10 yards (9 m) in width. The base of the sill has been downfaulted by several feet. About 25 yards (23 m) further on notice a dyke of quartz dolerite known as *Cat's Nick Dyke* which cuts through the sandstone and teschenite sill.

Before continuing downhill, observe the classic Crag and Tail feature as demonstrated by the Castle Rock and the Royal Mile, and the Calton Hill and Regent Road.

You have now completed your excursion over Holyrood Park and have returned to the starting point.

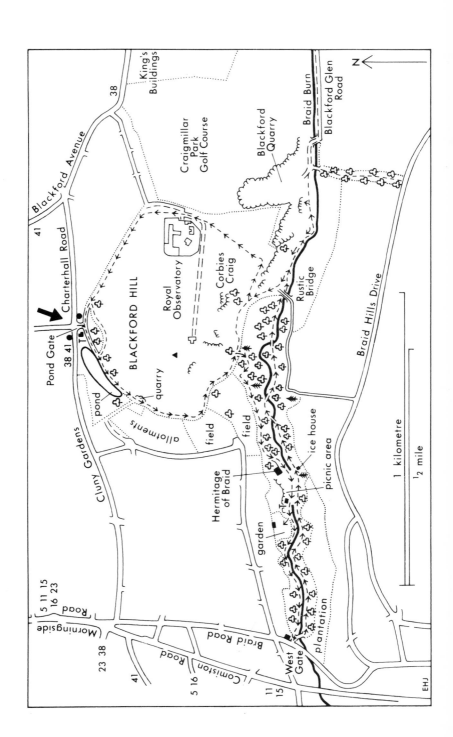

Walk 2: Blackford Hill and Hermitage of Braid

Starting Point   This circular walk begins at the east entrance to the Blackford Pond area in Cluny Gardens (Edinburgh Corporation bus service Nos 41 and 38 pass this gate and there is a small car park).

Distance   3 miles (4.8 km)

The plantation opposite the gate on the slope of Blackford Hill is mainly of Silver Birch, but it also contains some Rowan, Hawthorn, young Sycamore trees and farther up the hill some evergreen Norway Spruce. The undergrowth which is not very thick is formed of Elder and Bramble. This little wood provides a good shelter and feeding place for small passerine (perching) birds. In spring, which is the best time to look for woodland birds, you may see here, for example, Chaffinches and Blue Tits which are fairly common in this area; the migrant Willow Warbler, with its sweet descending song; the Great Tit which can be identified by its black 'zip-fastener' down the breast and, occasionally, flocks of pink-flanked Long-Tailed Tits, or Redpolls with their distinctive 'chi-chi-chit' flight call.

Turn right towards the pond. To the right of the path is a plantation of Sycamore and wych elm with undergrowth of bushes, chiefly Laurel and Holly. This is a favourite type of ground for foraging Blackbirds.

Keep on the path passing round the south side of Blackford Pond. Alder and Willow trees, which prefer a damp situation, fringe the edge of the pond. The Willow group of trees is difficult as many hybrids occur. At least two kinds occur here, one the Crack Willow which in spring has pale orange shoots with long pointed cone-shaped buds from which emerge in April yellow-green lance-shaped leaves, very glossy on the upper surface; the other a variety of White Willow with darker twigs and leaves, also lance-shaped, some but not all with a covering of silky hairs giving a greyish-white colour. On the Pond itself there is a collection mainly of semi-domesticated Mallard. But one should not make the mistake of assuming that all of the Pond Waterfowl are tame. You may, for example, see black Coots with their white frontal shield and bill and Moorhen (which are also black, but have a red base to the bill). Both tend to swim with jerky or nodding movements. These and the Mallard have bred on the Pond, where a small artificial island has been constructed for nesting, although sometimes nest sites tend to be usurped by a pair of Mute Swans. Occasionally, in winter, there may perhaps be a Pochard with its russet head or a pair of Tufted Duck (the male is black and white) while gulls (Black-headed, Common or Herring) assemble to eat bread provided for the ducks. On summer evenings Swifts, Swallows and House Martins may be seen hawking for insects over the Pond or round the Hill. As you go round the side of the Pond, the hillside on the left becomes progressively steeper and bare of trees, although a few Beech, Sycamore and Elder grow at the foot of the slope. The more open areas above have been colonised by scrub plants, such as Bracken, Bramble and Whin which spreads to the top of the hill. Lady Fern is seen here and in summer at the side of the path, pink patches of Rosebay Willowherb.

In this more open situation there may be seen birds such as the Linnet, with its red forehead and breast; the brown-streaked Meadow Pipit or the Dunnock (or Hedge Sparrow). Less common birds such as the Magpie or (in summer) the Whitethroat may also be spotted. Just before the Pond Gate, on the right, is an interesting old hybrid Black Poplar tree. Its leaves are pointed and broadly wedge-shaped at the base. It has a trunk with grey-brown bark deeply furrowed into short ridges. Notice on the side nearest the pond that an Elder sapling has rooted in the bottom of one of the ridges, probably planted by a bird when brushing an elder seed from its beak. In April the ground below becomes strewn with reddish-purple male catkins which have fallen off the tree.

A few yards beyond the Pond Gate, on the left, there are the remains of a small quarry. Here can be seen the base of the lava flow which formed the Hill. Below there is another layer of stones embedded in ash. The rock outcrops found throughout the area are of tuffs or volcanic ash and of lavas of two kinds — one known as Blackford Hill andesite (an igneous rock related to granite but with smaller grains) and Braid Hill trachyte (an igneous rock related to basalt).

Now follow the main path round Blackford Hill leading upwards until the valley of the Hermitage of Braid comes into sight on the right. As you approach the 'Crag' side of the Blackford Hill the hillside becomes steeper. The 'Tail' end slopes down gently to the east of the Hill towards Craigmillar Golf Course and this will be seen more distinctly later in the walk, when you approach the Observatory. On the hillside are some old Hawthorn trees amongst Blackthorn scrub. These, together with allotments on the right, attract to their fruits in autumn and winter birds such as Bullfinches and Song Thrushes. The wall on the right of the path has become colonised by Ivy and various species of moss and lichens. At its foot there is a colony of Field Horsetail.

Beyond the allotments on the right, you will see that the open fields show signs of previous cultivation in their 'Ridge and Furrow' formation. At the end of this open space there are some good specimens of Beech and Sycamore trees, presumably planted as a shelter belt.

On the hill side of the path the scrub vegetation of Wild Rose, Whin (Gorse) and Elder increases. Here from July to September the Wood Sage is much in evidence.

In front, the rock formation known as 'Corbies Crag' comes into view. This was created by the advancing ice during the period of glaciation. Over this crag there are occasionally not only Crows or Jackdaws but a pair of Kestrels hovering and possibly hunting for small mammals.

Enter the Hermitage Estate through a gap in the wall on the right where the path reaches its highest point. Here is a tree-covered valley of the Braid Burn. During the last period of glaciation in Scotland about 20,000 years ago the whole area was covered by a thick mantle of ice, moving eastward. When the climate improved the ice sheet retreated northward, halting several times, and the melt waters of the glaciers cut out a deep drainage channel – a glacier outflow channel – now occupied by the Braid Burn as it runs eastward through the valley of the Hermitage of Braid.

Although today the woodland which covers the sides of the valley is mainly artificial the original woodland vegetation would have formed part of the Old Lothian Forest contemporary with the Caledonian Forest which was recognised to exist in Roman times. The woodland now consists of trees of four different ages – the oldest over 180 years, the next some 100 years or so old, next naturally regenerated Sycamore about 30 years old. Finally there have been more recent group plantings in clearings of Sycamore, Ash, Birch, and some Conifers.

Once you have passed through the gap in the wall make your way downhill keeping to the right and on the path which roughly follows the old fence dividing woodland from field. At the fork about 400 yards (360 m) from the gap take the track to the left which leads to the House. In the woodland area just after passing through the gap, notice that the trees on the shallower soil of the upper slope are chiefly of Beech. Because of the heavy shading of the beech canopy there is no shrub layer. The heavy clays of the bottom of the valley support a mixture of trees whose leaves cast less shade and in consequence, there is quite a thick shrub layer underneath them.

Walking through the woodland in spring you will see flowering, typical woodland herbaceous plants such as Moschatel, Wood Sanicle, Wood Sorrel, Wood Anemone, Dog's Mercury,

Enchanter's Nightshade and Barren Strawberry. Listen for the strident caws of a colony of Rooks nesting in the canopy of the higher trees, while such birds as the Starling, and the Green Woodpecker, with its 'yaffling' call-note nest in holes in the trunks of the older trees. In the spring also can sometimes be heard the trill of the Wood Warbler or a twittering 'charm' of Goldfinches in the tree-tops. In hard winters the good feeding among the tree roots and beech masts may attract large flocks of brightly-coloured Bramblings, winter visitors to our country from Scandinavia.

The House of Hermitage of Braid   The Hermitage of Braid, which you approach from the rear, and the Estate itself have an interesting history. From about the 12th century there were castles in this area built by the powerful Barons of Braid; but these were situated on the crags above the present house. There was also an earlier mansion house known as 'The Hermitage' (a word which is said to indicate that at that place originally was a hermit's cell) built on the Burn in the 18th century by the Browns of Braid. In 1631 the Estate was purchased by Sir William Dick, who later became Lord Provost of Edinburgh and was a zealous Covenanter.

The present house was probably designed by the Adam brothers (Robert Adam was responsible for the design of much of Edinburgh's New Town). The building was completed in 1785 by Charles Gordon of Cluny who had married a daughter of the Laird of Mortonhall. Gordon arranged with his father-in-law to exchange the four acres of ground comprising the Dell behind the House for part of his Braid Estate. He planted trees in the Dell, levelled the front lawn, and demolished the old Corn Mill, which was on the Burn about 150 yards in front of the House. (To this mill, the farmers of Braid had taken their grain to be ground; an old millstone may still be seen a few yards above the waterfall west of the House.)

The Hermitage remained in the ownership of the Gordon family till 1868. Later residents included Sir John Skelton, a 19th-century advocate and historian, and C. G. Barkla, Professor of Natural Philosophy at Edinburgh University. In 1937, the Estate and House were purchased by the late Mr John McDougal, to be 'used as a Public Park and Recreation Ground for the benefit of Citizens'.

Lawn and the Burn beyond   Royal Fern, with its large leaves with their distinct spore-bearing parts, grows in a plot on the grass in front of the house. It has without doubt been planted, as this fern grows wild in Britain in only a few places in the west. In spring, over the lawn a Spotted Flycatcher may dart out from the surrounding trees, while a quick tapping may herald the arrival of a Great Spotted Woodpecker with a spectacular coat of black, white and red. Tree Creepers may be seen climbing the trunks of the trees in search of insects during the spring and summer, while in winter if the weather is hard one may even glimpse the bright blue flash of a passing Kingfisher. On the Burn itself, one may see if one is lucky (and very quiet) a couple of portly brown and white Dippers searching for underwater larvae.

The fresh water fauna in the Burn would merit a full investigation; during a short evening visit there were found in the

Figure 15

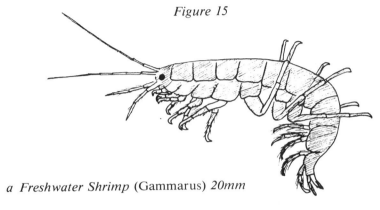

a Freshwater Shrimp (Gammarus) *20mm*

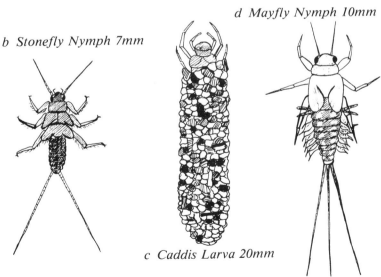

b Stonefly Nymph 7mm

d Mayfly Nymph 10mm

c Caddis Larva 20mm

Larva: a young insect which is different in appearance from the adult
Nymph: a young insect which is similar in appearance to the adult

water, Water Louse (*Asellus*) or Water Slater, Caddis larvae, Midge larvae (*Chironomids*), Flatworms, Mayfly nymphs, Leech and River Limpet (see Figure 15, c, d, e, f, g, h). Several Brown Trout were seen.

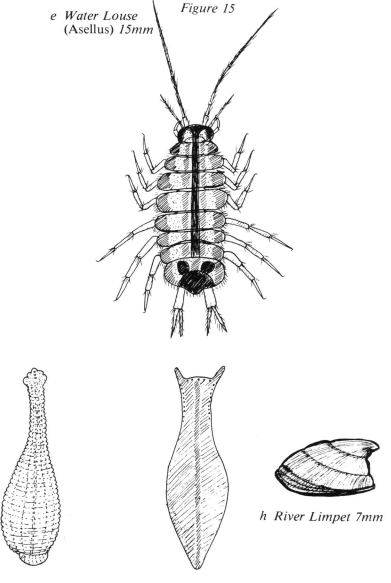

Figure 15

e *Water Louse*
(Asellus) *15mm*

h River Limpet 7mm

f Leech 15mm

g Flatworm (Polycelis) *15mm*

Continue westward along the north side on the right hand path of the Braid Burn (past the public toilets on the right) until a stile is reached near the west gate. Passing along the burn on the north side you will come to an enclosed area which is all that remains of the old walled garden. At the top is a building which is an old 18th-century dovecot kept to provide pigeons for the larder. It has two separate chambers, each measuring 18 feet (5.5 m) in diameter on the ground and tapering to a few feet at the top. Inside there were 1965 pigeon holes, each about ten inches square. Within the garden area now grow grasses which are typical of those found on neutral soil (see pages 29-31). Although trees now 20-25 years old have been planted here plenty of light still reaches the ground layer allowing the grasses to flourish.

All over the area on either side of the path outside the garden Few-flowered Leek (an introduced plant with narrow light-green leaves) is widespread, and is mixed in places with patches of Ramsons — its native relative with wider, elliptical leaves. Much of the ground is ivy-covered.

Examine the edge of the Burn as you go towards the West Gate. You will see flowering plants, such as Water Forget-me-not, which like a wet situation as well as liverworts and mosses. There are some very good examples of Hart's Tongue Fern in the retaining wall of the Burn.

West Gate of the Hermitage   This marks the turning point of the walk and is the approximate site where the northerly retreat of the ice was temporarily arrested (as described in Part I). The gatehouse was originally an old tollhouse which in 1893 was removed from its original site in Morningside Road, near Jordan Burn, and rebuilt stone by stone at the Hermitage entrance. In the Lodge garden there is a good specimen of an Ash tree recognisable in spring by its black buds and by its drooping branches, with their upturned twigs.

Turn left across the stone bridge and follow the main path through the valley (again passing in front of the House) to the Rustic Bridge. Just over the bridge on the left there is an interesting series of old Oak trees including Sessile, Pedunculate and Turkey. In the undergrowth, chiefly of Holly and Rhododendron, you may see such birds as the Wren 'chipping' at the intrusion on its territory or perhaps a tiny Goldcrest — the smallest British bird — as well as Bullfinches, Chaffinches, Robins, Blackbirds and Song Thrushes. On the hilly ground to the right of the path you will see a plantation of trees, mostly Scots Pine, but with some deciduous trees such as Flowering Cherry and Horse Chestnut amongst them. The age of the Pine may be told by the number of whorls of branches given off from the main axis of the tree.

On the sides of the path woodland plants are well represented. In spring look out for Golden Saxifrage, Wood Sanicle, Wood Sorrel, Wood Avens (Herb Bennet), Wood Anemone, and in particular the carpets of Celandine and more Few-flowered Leek. You will also see patches of Spring Beauty.

On the south bank nearly opposite the House is a short path, about 11 yards (10 m) long leading up to the old Ice House which was used for the preservation of food in summer before the days of refrigerators. (The Ice House can be seen from the main path.)

Past the house the sloping valley narrows, and the banks become steeper. As the melt waters of the glacier caused erosion, the walls of the gorge were disturbed and unbalanced, and blocks of the slumped trachyte were thrown up on either side. The commonest ground plants on the slopes are Broad Buckler-fern, mosses and liverworts. Here is a favourite summer haunt of the Grey Wagtail, with its yellow 'undercarriage'.

In the area past the first wooden bridge, even in winter, the Grey Squirrel may often be seen foraging among the trees or running swiftly along a branch. The more open area is a favourite feeding place for Blue, Great and Coal Tits, some of which will come to be fed by hand when other food is scarce.

Pass through the gate and walk under the Rustic Bridge — follow the path on the north bank of the Burn. The ground here is more open. To the north is a high crag of Blackford Hill andesite, with a steep scree slope. On the south side of the Burn there is a step-like profile, the upper part of which was formed by ice erosion and the lower by melt water from the glacier.

The vegetation in this area is of low scrub, such as Broom, Whin, Rose and Elder with Willows by the Burn. Along the banks of the Burn in spring there is usually a large area of Giant Butterbur, a native of Eastern Russia, like other Butterburs in flower before the leaves are out. In summer Mimulus or Monkeyflower and a species of Water Crowfoot flourish in the Burn.

The slopes of the hill are frequented by such birds as Bullfinches, Yellowhammers and Linnets, while in winter one may see on the opposite grassy slopes winter visitors such as Fieldfares and Redwings.

Old Quarry After going through the iron gate in the stone wall, on the left there is an old quarry in which there are veins of andesite, and here minerals such as reddish jasper and translucent bluish-white chalcedony (a mixture of quartz and opal) may also be found. At the entrance to the quarry stands the Agassiz Rock (marked by a small plaque), where the famous Swiss geologist, Louis Agassiz, found grooves on the cliff face and in the cave below and deduced that these were caused by the land ice — however, later opinions have been expressed that they may have been made by earth movement or by under-cutting by glacier melt water.

Retrace your steps for a short distance and climb steps to the right of the Rustic Bridge. The track marks the outcrop of eroded tuff, which separates the Blackford Hill andesite from the Braid Hill trachyte.

Halfway up the hillside leave the main track and follow a path (not the first one) to the right which passes over the shoulder of the hill to the Royal Observatory. On the way up or perhaps further on in summer you may hear the song of a Skylark or see a small bird with a black head and white collar and a rich chestnut breast perched on top of a whin bush. This is a Stonechat and, if alarmed, it will probably start up scolding 'Wheet, tsack, tsack', like two stones being hit together. This is a typical bird of gorse-clad territory, as is the Linnet.

Pass to the right of the Observatory. Here you are crossing the 'Tail' part of the 'Crag and Tail' formation. Look towards the north and you will see the Castle Hill, the Calton Hill and Arthur's Seat and Salisbury Crags.

Follow the path (ignoring the road down to the right) which leads downwards past a plantation of trees including Elm, Sycamore and Silver Birch to the starting place at the Pond Gate.

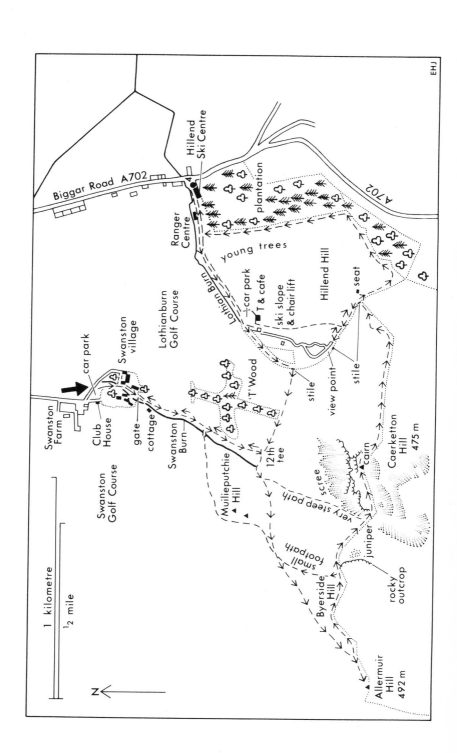

Walks 3a and 3b:
Pentland Hills

Starting Point   The starting point for these walks is the car park next to Swanston Golf Course Clubhouse. If not travelling by car a journey on a No. 4 or No. 32 bus to the top of Swanston Road, then a walk of about half a mile (800 m) down Swanston Road passing over the new roadway will take you to the starting point. When travelling towards Swanston village good views are seen of the 'T' Wood and the Pentland Hill top of Caerketton Hill. Caerketton Hill can be seen from a long distance away and it is easily identified by its rocky outcrop and scree slopes.

On either side of the road arable ground supports crops of barley, wheat, and potatoes. This ground was formed by soil being washed down from the hills thousands of years ago and settling in the valley.

Before reaching the car park, to the west of Swanston Farm, hidden by trees is the house where R. L. Stevenson spent his childhood days from 1867-1880. In summer look out for Swallows and House Martins flying about the farm buildings and fields. Around the farm buildings, Robins and Pied Wagtails can sometimes be seen searching for food.

Distance   Walk 3a — 1¼ miles (2 km) from Swanston car park to the top of Allermuir and back to Swanston village.

Walk 3b — 3½ miles (5.5 km) from Swanston car park via the top of Allermuir and Caerketton to the bus terminal on the A702. 4½ miles (7.25 km) for the complete walk back to Swanston village.

These walks cover rough ground and, especially 3b, are steep and stony in places. It is advisable to wear stout footwear and carry waterproof clothing. Dogs should be kept on a leash.

Both walks

Car park through Swanston village to edge of 'T' Wood   From the car park take the path to the east end. This leads through a small wood, over Swanston Burn up towards the village. The wood is a mixed plantation chiefly of Sycamore, Ash, Wych Elm and Lime trees. Notice the Wellingtonia or Giant Sequoia with reddish, spongy bark and cords of scale-like foliage leaves. These are lost from the lower branches probably owing to the closeness of the other trees. The undergrowth in the wood in made up of bushes of Yew, Holly, Elder and Snowberry — a bush introduced into British gardens from Western America early in the 19th century. It has now spread widely in woods and on waste ground. In spring the herbaceous plants seen flowering are those typical of a mixed moist wood and include Lesser Celandine, Wood Avens (Herb Bennet), Wild Hyacinth and Few-flowered Leek, a plant introduced into Britain which is now found in many woody areas of Edinburgh. It will be seen on five of the walks described. Listen for the 'zi-zi-zi' of the Goldcrest.

Swanston village   The village contains four groups of thatched cottages which were built in the 18th century and some years ago were renovated and rethatched by Edinburgh Corporation as it was then called. There is an old schoolhouse in the village which served the community in the past. There are other terraced cottages which are occupied by farm workers but these were built at a later date than the thatched cottages.

Continue uphill on the road which the path joins, past the old white schoolhouse and the white thatched cottages, noticing the fine examples of Yew, Wych Elm, Horse Chestnut, Scots Pine, and Crack Willow next to the Burn on the way. When you come to a gate go through it, noticing the English Elms on the right. Compare them with the Wych Elms seen a little earlier. After about 50 yards (46 m) bear left to continue on the track up the left side of the Burn. On the left is the Lothianburn Golf Course, on the right Swanston Golf Course. On the right of the Burn is another thatched cottage standing on its own. Scottish Blackface Sheep will be seen grazing on the hills.

Pause to look at the marshy land at the Burn's edge, where you will see Rushes and other plants which like a wet situation, including Brooklime, Water-cress, Water Mint, Water Forget-me-not and, flowering as early as April, Golden Saxifrage, also seen on the Hermitage Walk in the damp parts of the wood. Water animals, such as Flatworms, Caddis larvae and Stonefly nymphs may be seen resting on stones in the burn (see Figure 15c, b, g).

The grassy track—grasses on the side of the track are mainly Common Bent, Wavy Hair-grass, Sheep's Fescue and Creeping Soft-grass—now passes between Whin bushes which in spring are covered in yellow flowers. (Amongst the grass there are many clumps of Foxglove with both red and white flowers—a plant which is common on acid grassland.) These bushes, which can be seen growing on both golf courses, make very good nesting sites for birds such as Dunnock, Robin, Blackbird, Song Thrush, Yellowhammer, Linnet and Wren, also an occasional Stonechat can be seen. The fairways and rough areas of the golf courses form another habitat for birds like the Meadow Pipit, Skylark and Lapwing. The Lapwing nests in the fields in the spring and the

Meadow Pipit and Skylark nest in the longer grass surrounding the golf courses.

Continue up the path until you reach the edge of the 'T' Wood on your left. The 'T' Wood, as it is known, is in fact a cross, as can be seen from the air. It is mainly of Beech with a few Scots Pine. There is very little undergrowth in it as it is heavily grazed by sheep. Not many birds nest in it apart from the Tit family and Starlings which nest in holes in the trees and Crows which nest on top of the trees. In the spring a male Cuckoo can usually be heard singing in the wood from quite a distance away. Trees seen growing near the burn are Wych Elm, Birch, Rowan and Alder.

Edge of 'T' Wood to the top of Allermuir Hill From the end of the 'T' Wood continue up main path to end of stone dyke (12th tee), bear right taking the path which leads off uphill (passing the very steep path to Caerketton Hill) with Muilieputchie Hill (see map) on your right. The path now takes you into a different habitat of mainly Mat grass with varying cover of Fescues, Bent and Wavy-hair grasses. There follow areas covered with Heather (Ling), Bell Heather and Bilberry. Notice the moss growing amongst the Heather and the greyish-green lichens on the ground and attached to the heather stems.

On this main path continue uphill to the top of Allermuir (1617 feet/492 m) crossing a small footpath on the way (see map). From the top of the hill on a clear day can be seen marvellous views of the surrounding countryside. To the north-west the Forth Railway and Road bridges and the Ochil Hills and the mountains beyond; to the north the Lomond Hills; to the east the Forth coast and the gannetery of the Bass Rock, a volcanic plug, and the pointed hill of North Berwick Law, another volcanic plug. To the south, the hills of the Moorfoots and to the south-west most of the peaks of the Pentlands can be seen.

The above points can be seen on the Indicator erected near the top of Allermuir by the National Trust for Scotland in 1961.

Walk 3a — Allermuir Hill back to Swanston Village

From the top of the hill you may return to Swanston Village the way you walked up or walk down the slope beside the fence towards Caerketton Hill until you see the Juniper growing (see Walk 3b), then retrace your steps until you come to the small footpath which will lead you downhill to the main path leading back to the village. (You crossed this path while following the main path to the top of Allermuir.)

Walk 3b — From Allermuir Hill to Caerketton (1550 feet/473 m)

From the top of Allermuir Hill retrace footsteps down the hill until you come to the 'Y' junction of the footpaths. Keep to the path on the right which runs along the north side of the wire fence. Continue along this path past the rocky outcrops of Byreside Hill and past a large patch of Juniper bushes on the south side of the fence. Juniper is one of our three native Conifers (the others are Scots Pine and Yew) and here it is a remnant of the natural Juniper that once covered a widespread area of the Pentlands. It has whorls of awl-shaped tapering needles and berry-like cones. Near the patch of Juniper there are masses of Bilberry, a deciduous spreading shrub with angular stems and Crowberry, a trailing evergreen shrub both of which are mentioned under Upland Heath in the Introduction (see page 3).

After a while the path joins up with the very steep one which comes up from Swanston Village. Carry on and climb uphill past the rocky outcrops on the top of Caerketton where there is a small stone cairn built up over the years by passing walkers. From the top, once again, very good views can be seen of Edinburgh and the surrounding areas. Care should be taken on the top of Caerketton Hill not to wander too far away from the footpath as there are steep grassy slopes above rock faces.

Top of Caerketton to Hillend Park   From the top of Caerketton Hill continue going eastward along the path descending, then ascending on to the hill above the ski slope. On the east of Caerketton Wild Thyme, Heath Bedstraw and Sheep's Sorrel, plants typical of acid grassland, are common.

Continue along the path and descend from the hill on a steep slope, keeping close to the wire fence. At the bottom of the hill cross over the stile and continue past the hillock which has a wooden seat on top of it. At this stage there are many paths which wind their way through the Whin bushes and Bracken. (From the stile a detour may be made to the viewpoint above the ski slope — see map.) Bracken is one of the most widespread of all ferns. It is common on hill land, especially on light, well-drained acid soil and in woodlands. It spreads rapidly by underground stems (rhizomes), often invading good grassland — this may be attributed to the selective grazing habits of sheep — and it is quite difficult to eradicate. Although now there are certain chemicals being used in bracken control, the process is rather expensive as spraying is carried out by helicopter.

Take a path that goes eastward and descend until you come to a private plantation consisting of mixed deciduous trees and conifers, forming a shelter belt in the area.

The plantation is surrounded by a wire fence and you should turn left at the fence and follow the path which runs northwards until you come to the offices of the Pentland Hill Ranger Service.

Growing in the Lothian Burn, notice Monkeyflower (*Mimulus guttatus*) a plant introduced from North America in 1830. It has now spread into watery places throughout Britain.

You may like to end your walk here by turning right and following the road to the bus terminus on the A702. If returning to Swanston Village turn left and follow the road up to the main car park for the ski lift. At the car park keep to the right and follow the track beside the ski slope until you come to the stile. Near to the car park, areas have been fenced off and planted with young trees.

From Hillend Park to Swanston Village and car park   Cross over the stile by the side of the ski slope and follow the path running past the golf course and the 'T' wood until you come to the 12th tee. Turn right towards Swanston Village and retrace footsteps from the beginning of the walk through the village past the thatched cottages and the old schoolhouse until you come to the starting point at the car park.

Note   If you would like to go up on the chair lift, tickets are obtainable from the Ski Centre near the entrance to the Park, not at the ski slope. The Ranger Centre run by Lothian Regional Council should be visited for further information about the area.

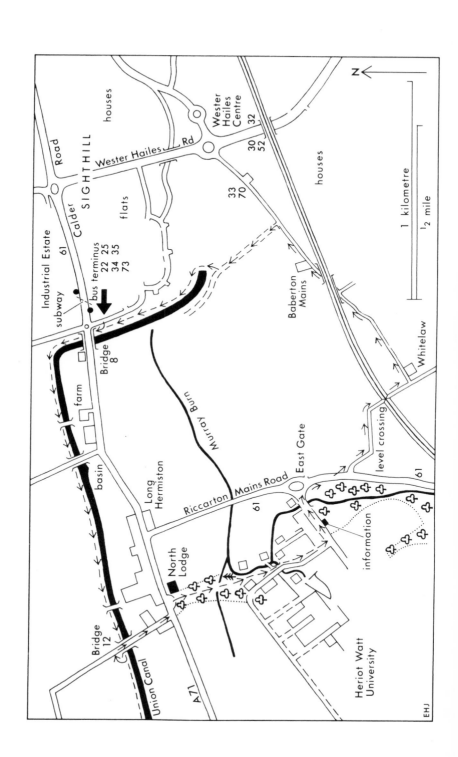

Walk 4: Along the Union Canal, through the Plantations of Heriot-Watt University Grounds at Riccarton and over Farmland on the Outskirts of the City.

Starting Point   Bus terminus on the Calder Road, Sighthill, which may be reached by bus Nos 22, 25, 34, 35. Car parking is without restriction in the side roads off Calder Road.

Distance   3¼ miles (5.25 km)

The bus terminus is at the City boundary, where the complex of modern flats and houses and the industrial estate of Sighthill stop abruptly giving way to the open farmland of Midlothian. Two hundred yards (180 m) further west lies the Union Canal, opened in 1822, linking Edinburgh to Glasgow and the West via Falkirk where the Union Canal joins the Forth and Clyde Canal. The canals continued as busy waterways until the coming of the railways after which trade steadily diminished and by 1933 all traffic had ceased. The old towpath has now become a pleasant walkway, and with relatively little disturbance and no grazing, the verges alongside the path are colourful for much of the summer with a wide variety of flowering plants. No rarities will be seen but the botanist will find it a rewarding area.

With no commercial traffic on the Canal for many years the slow-moving water has been colonised by freshwater vegetation providing a sheltered habitat for Mallard, Little Grebe (Dabchick) and Moorhen. Every few years dredging of parts of the Canal becomes necessary to prevent it becoming completely choked, and now allowing it to be used for boating.

After leaving the bus or parking the car, continue to walk out of Edinburgh for a further 200 yards (180 m) where the Canal will be seen passing under the road at Bridge 8. Scramble down onto the old towpath and start walking north with the Canal on your left. Keep to the towpath until Bridge 12 is reached.

The path keeps straight for 200 yards (180 m) before turning west. Do not be discouraged by the mud and dumped rubbish of this first short section as there is an immediate improvement as soon as the corner is turned. Reed Sweet-grass, which can be recognised by its very stout typically grass-shaped leaves, dominates the swamp zone of shallow water fringing the bank. It spreads its very strong underground stems. Farmland now lies on either side of the Canal and the birdlife associated with it is good, particularly in winter when flocks of Golden Plover and Lapwing are usually in the fields and flights of Fieldfare and Redwing are common.

To the north-east, Corstorphine lies about 3 miles (5 km) distant, a wooded hilly public park within the City Boundary. The Lomond Hills of Fife are to the north, and on any clear day the long stretch of the Ochil Hills lying behind Dollar and Tillicoultry can be seen.

Much of the hedge has been lost but typical hedgerow birds frequent the area including Yellowhammer and Goldfinch. Shrubs of Downy and Dog Rose and small scrub trees provide shelter and cover for the birds as well as giving colour and variety to the scene.

On pages 29 and 30 some of the grasses most likely to be found on non-acidic soils are illustrated. Grasses are very well represented on the walk and with the aid of the drawings identification may be made of some of these.

Bridges 9 and 10 are close together. As you pass under notice the grooves worn in the corner stones by the tow ropes of the barges. During the summer months Swallows will be seen flying over the farm buildings at Bridge 9.

Flowering plants are abundant and in summer very colourful on either side of the pathway. They include Valerian, Meadowsweet, Great Willowherb and Water Forget-me-not in the waterlogged soil near the edge of the Canal and Meadow Vetchling, Garlic Mustard (Jack-by-the-Hedge) and flowering later in the summer, Common Knapweed (Hardheads) amongst the less wet grass higher up the bank. At the back of the book there is a list of other plants which can be found.

At Bridge 10 the Canal widens to form a basin. These basins occur at intervals along the length of the Canal to allow room for barges to turn and also to provide places for loading and unloading. At the basin the structure of the Canal walls can be seen — a straight face of solid blocks of stone. Because of this there is an abrupt change from the vegetation of the bank to the plants growing in the water and a complete absence of vegetational zoning as explained on page 32.

The amount of vegetation seen in the open water of the Canal varies from year to year depending on how recently dredging has taken place. Usually much in evidence in this part of the Canal is Common Duckweed, a floating plant which grows in a mass. Each plant consists of one small light-green leaf not more than two-tenths of an inch (6 mm) in diameter. A single root dangles into the water from its lower surface, acting as a kind of balancer. Floating Pondweed, a plant rooted to the bottom is also likely to be present here. It has browny-green oval leaf blades which float on the water's surface at the end of long flexible leaf stalks. It produces a stalk of green flowers which projects above the surface.

From between Bridges 10 and 11 the superstructure of the two Forth Bridges can be seen, and rather more to the west notice the pinkish hue of the old shale bings of West Lothian, a present day reminder of the once flourishing shale oil and paraffin industry. These bings overlie deposits of Burdiehouse limestone. (Limestones are sedimentary rocks formed under water, usually salt, from shells of animals which lived in the water. Burdiehouse limestone is an example of a limestone which formed under fresh water).

Along the banks wherever there is tall vegetation at the water's edge giving a suitable breeding habitat, watch for the brilliant colour of damselflies.

Before leaving the Canal at Bridge 12 you will have had several fine views of the Pentland Hills lying to the south of Edinburgh. You will also have passed two of the old half-mile stones beside the towpath giving the distance to Edinburgh on one face and to Falkirk on the other. You will also have seen how the diversity of plant life is able to support a good variety of insects, including moths and butterflies, thereby attracting insect-eating birds while the autumn seeds and fruits support flocks of Finches. The shelter along the banks of the water provides a habitat for freshwater birds.

Leave the Canal at Bridge 12, walk over the bridge and up past the cottages to the main road (A71). Obliquely across the main road is the pedestrian entrance to the grounds of Heriot-Watt University.

The new University of Heriot-Watt was given the grounds of Riccarton by Midlothian County Council in 1966 and the University was opened by its first Chancellor, Sir Alec Douglas Home, in 1969. The building programme is not yet complete so part of the University land continues to be used for farming. Last century, Riccarton was a private estate when the foundation of the present grounds was laid. Avenues of trees were planted as well as many specimen trees scattered through the grounds. Lawns and gardens were planned and a small loch established. Great care has been taken by the University authorities in the siting of buildings and in the landscaping to keep as much of the amenity of the estate as practicable. Tree felling has been kept to a minimum and new plantings of both conifers and hardwoods have been made.

Enter the grounds of Riccarton by the North entrance gates off the A71, walk the length of the driveway and continue on the pathway past the car parks until you come to the East driveway. At the North entrance gate is the Lodge, with its ornamental chimneys and carved woodwork under the eaves. The heavy roof slates are arranged to form a simple decorative pattern. The entrance drive is flanked on either side by a shelter belt with an avenue of Limes bordering the road and Sycamores the perimeter. The depth of the shelter belt is made up of a variety of trees and shrubs amongst which Rhododendrons, Yew and Holly are conspicuous. The trees are tall and well grown, many having reached maturity so the canopy is no longer open except in those parts where clearings have been made. However, in the spring, before the leaves are on the trees some of the early woodland flowers such as Lesser Celandine, Primrose and Snowdrop can be seen. Some clearings have been replanted with Larch, Beech and Scots Pine and some of the young trees show damage to the bark caused by Roe Deer. Roe Deer used to be seen crossing this driveway quite frequently but in recent years they have preferred quieter parts of the estate where disturbance is less.

After a few hundred yards, the orderly avenue of Limes gives way to more erratic planting of trees and greater variety, including Horse Chestnut, Ash, Rowan, Beech, Birch, Elm and Walnut. The evergreens are represented by Scots Pine, Austrian Pine and a very tall Western Hemlock. Beside the Hemlock the ground is boggy and Dogwood has been planted here, the red twigs being very conspicuous and colourful in winter. Young Alders are also growing in this damp habitat.

Close to the driveway runs the Murray Burn, changing its direction at a junction of roads and paths. At this point there is an opportunity to compare some of the different Willow species. Two of the narrow-leaved Willows are growing in the hedge and the wide-leaved Goat Willow is close by.

The impact of nearby buildings has been softened by mixed plantings of Beech, Pine, Larch and Rhododendron along with taller Sycamores. The effect is pleasing at any time of the year while in winter the brown wrinkled beech leaves contrast well with the evergreens.

Dense hedges have been planted to screen the large car parks and contain an attractive mixture of Beech, Hawthorn, Field Maple and Hornbeam. Already these hedges are providing good winter shelter and spring nesting places for many hedgerow birds. The hedges remain colourful through autumn and winter, with the Maples giving autumn colour and the young Beeches retaining their leaves through the winter months.

Turn left into the East driveway and walk along it to leave the grounds of Riccarton by the main entrance (East gate) to the University immediately past the car parks. These car parks may be used by the public, and for those without cars there is a public bus service to the City centre, details of which can be obtained from the porters' building in the drive. This driveway, like the earlier one, is flanked by tall rows of Limes under which carpets of Ramsons (Wood Garlic) flower in spring. Behind the porters' building, where there is another car park, stood a pinetum where Wellingtonias were planted last century. There is one close to the exit gates probably around 100 years old.

As you walk along the drive notice the high rise flats of Sighthill ahead of you with Edinburgh Castle and Rock just to the right, followed by Arthur's Seat and Salisbury Crags, described in Walk 1. Craiglockhart Hill, craggy, smaller and rather nearer is slightly further to the right. On the other side of the high rise flats the low wooded sweeping rise of Corstorphine Hill almost obscures one of the twin peaks of the Fife Lomond Hills.

After you leave Riccarton Estate and Heriot-Watt University grounds by the East gate turn right and walk about 200 yards (about 180 m) up the road and turn into a very minor road on your left.

The final part of the walk passes through fertile farmland. All over the country good farmland is constantly being sacrificed to the needs of urban expansion. Here the building has been halted at the City Boundary, which, for a short distance runs along the line of the Canal.

As the road levels out a broad expanse of low-lying fields reaching the City Boundary comes into view. These fields are usually used for crops; they are relatively sheltered and are often amongst the earliest to be harvested in the area. Wheat, barley and hay are the most usual crops. Two crops of hay may be taken off a field in a single season for conversion into silage which is used for the winter feeding of cattle. If this is being done regularly, fertiliser will probably be put on the field each year. Wheat sown in the autumn, known as winter wheat, is ready for harvesting in the summer earlier than the spring sown wheat. The different conditions under which the two crops have grown and ripened produce differences in the flour that is milled from them, in general the winter wheat producing the softer flour.

Hedges still remain on the landscape but many have been removed for greater farming efficiency including in all probability one on the left side of the road. An old hedge of Hawthorn and Beech still stands on the other side, however; seldom more than 4 feet (1.3 m) high but with thick gnarled stems indicating considerable age and repeated cutting over the years. All the fields on higher ground and with less shelter are being used as pasture for sheep and cattle, often with both in the same field for the cattle eat the taller grasses, encouraging the growth of shorter turf which is preferred by sheep.

From this higher road a much wider view north can be seen than was possible from the Canal towpath. The two Forth bridges are readily picked out but the widely spaced twin peaks of the Fife Lomonds are often obscured by haze. The Pentland Hills lie to the south (see page 17 and walks 3a and 3b). Torphin Quarry on the north side of the Pentlands shows clearly, particularly in evening light. Stone is quarried here for the igneous rock, basalt, and used for road making.

The road leads up to and over a railway level crossing. This is the main Edinburgh-Carlisle line with many trains passing throughout the day. As the line is on a curve, visibility is reduced, so please *listen* and look both ways before crossing and keep children close beside you. The road turns left at Whitelaw Farm. Keep to the road past the entrance to Baberton House, and then under the railway line and on to the reconstructed farm complex of Baberton Mains.

After you have crossed the railway, you will see that the hedges are no longer being cut. This could be to increase the shelter for the beasts. Along the hedge running beside the railway line, cattle have been browsing the hedge, trimming it well back up to about five feet.

Round Whitelaw Farm the surface of the entrances has been improved with a layer of the waste material from the shale bings. From Whitelaw Farm the route continues downhill for the rest of the walk, at first with Baberton Golf Course on the right separated from the road by a belt of mature trees including Oak, Ash, Beech, Wych Elm, some younger Sycamores and Hawthorn. The hedge to the left of the road is mainly of Hawthorn with Elderberry and Rose amongst it.

Baberton Mains has been beautifully reconstructed and restored, the old farm buildings now forming several private houses with pantile roofs and attractive gardens, all in sharp contrast with the modern high flats now close at hand. The reconstruction received a Saltire Award in 1975.

To cater for the many dwellers in the area, allotment gardens have recently been made across the road from Baberton Mains. There still remains a small field as yet unused which is a typical example of neglected ground with Ragwort growing rampant. This plant is the foodplant of the Cinnabar Moth caterpillar.

Watch carefully for the little track which is a right of way, leaving the road halfway between Baberton Mains and the high flats. This track cuts through an arable field to its boundary at the Canal. Cross over the Canal where it is culverted and continue up to the main road and the Sighthill bus terminus.

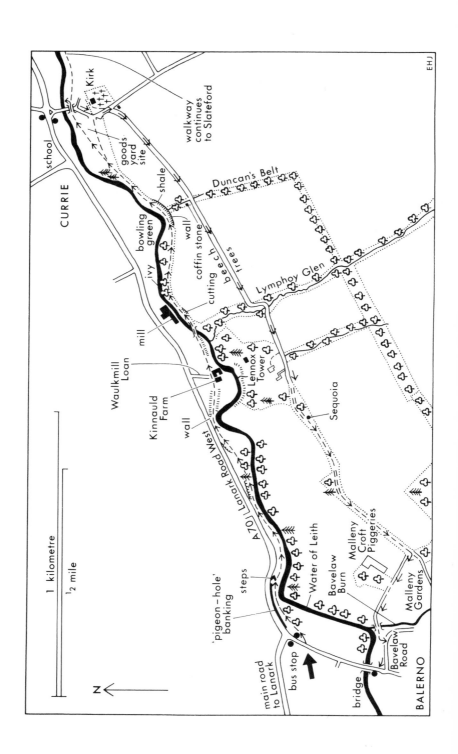

1 kilometre
½ mile

N ←

EHJ

CURRIE

school

Kirk

goods
yard
site

walkway
continues
to Slateford

shale

Duncan's Belt

bowling green

ivy

wall

coffin stone

cutting

beech

trees

Lymphoy Glen

mill

Waulkmill
Loan

Kinnauld
Farm

wall

Lennox
Tower

Sequoia

A70 Lanark Road West

Water of Leith

'pigeon-hole'
banking

steps

Bavelaw
Burn

Malleny
Croft
Piggeries

Malleny
Gardens

main road
to Lanark

bus stop

bridge

Bavelaw
Road

BALERNO

Walk 5: Balerno—Currie—Balerno, beside the Water of Leith and along the old railway line

Starting Point This walk begins at the footpath at Balerno entered from Bridge Road a hundred yards (90 m) nearer the village than the bus stop of Nos 52, 53 Balerno, Eastern Scottish bus, but it is circular and can be commenced from several other access points. The line of the old railway is followed eastwards as far as Currie, where you take to the public road for a 100 yards (90 m) or so, then on to a private road which runs westward roughly parallel to, but at a higher elevation than, the outward path.

Distance 3¼ miles (5.25 km)

The Balerno Branch Railway was opened in 1874 as a single-line loop from the old Caledonian Railway at Slateford, and was in use until 1968, though passenger traffic was discontinued in 1943. Now it forms part of the Water of Leith Walkway commenced by Edinburgh Corporation in 1973, and many of the small bridges, retaining walls and cuttings will be noticed in the course of this walk.

The path leads downhill to the level of the Water of Leith. There is a fine border on the left of deciduous trees with bushes beneath, and in spring carpets of yellow Celandine flowers. On the moister edges of the area as well as on the sides of much of the route to be followed are large expanses of Butterbur whose spikes of male flowers push through the bare ground early in the year to be followed by very large rhubarb-like leaves. The plant spreads vegetatively as in the area there are no female flowers to set seed. Bright yellow flower heads of Coltsfoot, another plant which flowers in early spring before the leaves are out, is present in large patches.

Balerno to Currie Continue to follow the path. A short way along you will come to an even more recent man-made habitat in the shape of high concrete 'pigeon-hole' banking supporting a re-alignment of the Lanark Road. The base has been planted with Willow, Cotoneaster and Broom and the top with Honeysuckle, but natural colonisation even of the inhospitable pebble-filled niches has already begun with grasses, and Ivy spreading from the top and wind or bird-carried seeds of Dandelion, Groundsel,

Coltsfoot, Willowherb, Thistle, Dock and Clover making a start to the cycle of regeneration. These first rather stunted specimens will die and decay and the humus formed will provide nutrients for the next generation. Slowly nature will adopt this very barren soil. (Access to Lanark Road by steps at north end of the wall.)

Continue along the path for 200 yards (180 m) or so and it will be seen that the soil is moister and the vegetation lusher. Common hedgerow plants such as Red Campion, Jack-by-the-Hedge or Garlic Mustard and Cow Parsley are joined by such species as Bistort, Sweet Cicely, much Butterbur and later the water-loving Water Avens. Here and elsewhere on the walk a clear view of the river can be obtained, and a watch should be kept for two of the birds associated with running water, the Dipper and the Grey Wagtail. The Dipper may be noticed flying fast and straight only a foot or two above the water, or standing on a rock in mid-stream, white breast conspicuous, displaying its characteristic bobbing motion. Its single-note call is uttered in flight, but it has an attractive little song which it continues to use even in midwinter when few other birds can be heard. The Grey Wagtail may also be seen on this walk. It is seldom found far from running water where it busily searches out insects along the stream edge or flutters up to catch them in mid-air.

The path, which clearly follows the old railway track, now runs between wooded banks, the one on the right sloping to the river with open fields beyond. The vegetation is typical hedgerow/woodland with ground cover of Dog's Mercury, Ramsons with its strong smell of garlic, Goose-grass and Wood Avens. A closer examination of some of the last-mentioned plants will reveal that they are in fact hybrids between the nodding pink-flowered Water Avens (*Geum rivale*) and the smaller upright yellow-flowered Wood Avens or Herb Bennet (*Geum urbanum*).

All along this first stretch of the walk, much of it edged by scrubby vegetation, the Lanark Road and houses bordering it are never far away and with the exception of Dipper and Yellow Wagtail, the birds likely to be seen and heard are the familiar garden birds—Blackbird, Starling, House Sparrow, Chaffinch, Song Thrush, Dunnock, Great Tit, Blue Tit and Robin.

Three hundred yards (275 m) or so after you pass the end of the wooded area you come to Kinnauld Farm, between the path and the water. It is the site of the old waulk-mill of Ballernoch, dating back to 1376, where woollen cloth was cleansed and finished by the fullers. In the 19th century it became a distillery, and only about the beginning of this century it changed its use yet again to a farm. Currently it is a piggery. (Access to Lanark Road.)

Continue to the wooden bridge over the Water of Leith about

100 yards (91 m) ahead, and cross over it. Just below it on the right hand side is a large clump of Ramsons and nearer the water is an attractive patch of Pink Purslane, an introduced plant from North America which has spread in the district in recent years. Higher up the bank is a fallen Elm tree on which grows the fungus Dryad's Saddle or Scaly Polypore (*Polyporus squamosus*) forming in the summer and early autumn tiers of semi-circular or fan-shaped straw-coloured caps. Look at the pores on the under surface of a cap. In these, the spores or reproductive cells of the fungus are formed. (The caps usually decompose during the winter, but new caps will probably appear in the same place the following year.) It is worthwhile looking at dead or dying trees to see if there are other fungi which have found a niche in rotting wood.

You have now moved into a quieter area where in May and June the songs of some of our summer visitors — Willow Warbler, Whitethroat, and possibly Garden Warbler and Blackcap — may be heard.

A short distance beyond the bridge the track has been cut through a rocky outcrop of shale. The banks on either side support trees, chiefly Elm and Sycamore.

Beyond the trees about 90 yards (80 m) from the bridge, on the right hand side, is a stand of Blackthorn. The white blossom of the Blackthorn in early summer precedes the growth of its leaves; in late autumn it produces the small bitter sloes. This can be compared with the much more abundant Hawthorn, whose white or less frequently pink blossom in June appears after the bushes are fully leaved, to be followed by the clusters of red haws much favoured by birds as autumn and winter food.

The path now runs beside a rich bank on the right of Meadow-sweet and Crane's-bill, with Water Avens indicating a moist soil. On the left between the path and the river there is a deciduous wood with some of the trees strangled by ivy. At the side of the path in this area you may see Field Horsetail. (Horsetails belong to a very primitive group of plants which flourished in the swamps of the Carboniferous Period over 200 million years ago at the time when the Coal Measures were being laid down. The ancient species were large — up to 100 feet (30 m) in height — woody tree-like plants; the living forms are non-woody perennials.)

Further on the path passes through another cutting with stone-retaining walls where rock climbing used to be practised, followed by another rocky outcrop of shale. The trees, chiefly Elms, Ash and Sycamore, on the bank above the stonefacing and the shale outcrop, give shade providing a cool, damp habitat for ferns, such as Male Fern and Broad Buckler-fern. Beyond the cutting and trees on the right there is another Blackthorn stand, larger than the one passed earlier.

On the left of the path, between the path and the water is a private woodland, mainly of introduced Norway Spruce, and here Coal Tits may be heard, their 'teechew' call similar to that of the Great Tit but higher and thinner in tone. It is possible in the course of this walk to see four species of the tit family — Blue Tit, Great Tit, Coal Tit and Long-tailed Tit — but although all of them are resident species only the first two can one be confident of seeing at any time of the year.

Examine the open ground of the Currie goods yard to which you now come. There is much Butterbur and Lesser Celandine carpeting large areas, and some plants not native of Britain, such as Cherry Laurel and Japanese Knotweed, have invaded. There is a Domesticated Apple bush which has probably grown from a seed of a cultivated tree.

Cross the railway bridge over the road, go down the steps to the left, turn left on to the road and walk under the bridge up the hill past Currie Kirk. There is a public path back to Balerno on the right, but pass that and take a Private Road beside a cottage, opposite the entrance to the graveyard.

Currie to Balerno   This is a typical country road bordered by hawthorn hedges, with arable fields beyond and with a rich flora in the verges. There are no rarities but a good succession of flowering, probably at the best in early summer. Abundant here and elsewhere in the Lothians but not widespread in Britain is the Few-flowered Leek introduced from the Caucasus, a member of the onion family as will be plain from its smell when it is crushed.

Edging the roadway amongst the grass are Dandelion, Daisy, Lesser Celandine, Germander Speedwell, Ribwort Plantain, Bush Vetch and on the damper ground nearer the hedge a profusion of Umbellifers each flowering in its time, such as Sweet Cicely, Cow Parsley, Ground-elder and Hogweed, together with Red Campion, Lady's-mantle, Stinging Nettle and Clovers. Ivy covers much of the ground. The thick plant cover, the hawthorn hedges and the holes in isolated Elm and Ash trees provide suitable nesting places for Dunnock, Chaffinch, Starling, Blackbird, Blue Tit, Great Tit and Whitethroat.

The road crosses a small belt of mixed woodland and a stream and a few paces in on the right is an engraved stone with the inscription, 'In this small enclosure are a number of stone coffins of various dimensions. They were discovered in December 1820 and this stone was erected by the proprietor, General Thomas Scott of Malleny, in order to point out the spot and to facilitate the researches of the curious into such interesting relics of antiquity. Renewed by the District Council 1971.' The original stone, the words barely decipherable, lies behind the present erect one. Trees include Holly, Yew, Beech, Horse Chestnut, Lime and Elm.

Now the road runs through an avenue of Beeches, and it is immediately plain that the leaf mosaic of these trees shuts off much of the light from the ground beneath, and growth is much thinner than in the open areas you have just passed, leaving mainly perennials such as Dandelion, Stinging Nettle and some Umbellifers. From this stretch of road on a clear day excellent views may be obtained across the Firth of Forth.

On the left of the path, about 20 yards (18 m) before the small bridge, can be seen the two species of wild garlic growing together — the Few-flowered Leek already mentioned, with small bulbils mixed with rather creamy flowers, and the commoner Ramsons, with broad, deep green leaves and showy head of starry white flowers. Near the small bridge, Crosswort makes a striking yellow green patch, with Water Avens in the damper ground.

The belt of woodland, known as Lymphoy Glen, with a burn running through it, is soon reached. It supports a typical woodland flora, and forms a corridor for wildlife connecting the Water of Leith with the Pentlands. The trees, which include Ash, Sycamore, Elm, Beech, Gean and Elder, are not so closely spaced that they exclude the light, and there is a good ground cover of Lesser Celandine, Wood Sorrel, Bluebell, Primrose, Wood Anemone and Ground Ivy. There is no grazing by sheep or cattle, so seedlings and well-grown saplings of all these trees can be found. Again this is a self-supporting community with trees and herbaceous plants drawing nutrients from the soil, themselves providing food and shelter for the animal kingdom, whose members in turn assist pollination (insects) and seed dispersal (birds and mammals). Bacteria and fungi bring about decay of dead matter and help in the recycling.

The Beech Avenue continues to the iron gates of Lennox House through which may be glimpsed the ivy-covered ruins of Lennox Tower. On the left of the path there is a belt of trees forming another corridor towards the Pentlands. The burn running through it continues through the grounds of Lennox House to the Water of Leith.

Beyond the gate about 60 yards (55 m) further on a strip of woodland on the left of the path must have been planted at the end of the last century with a variety of native and introduced trees — Scots Pine, Beech, Birch, Pedunculate Oak, Lime, Hornbeam, Horse Chestnut, Sycamore and towards the far end of the wood a Wellingtonia. This last tree, also called Giant Sequoia, is easily identified by its tall tapering trunk, covered with thick fibrous red-brown bark. It is warm and spongy to touch, and one of our native birds, the Tree Creeper, has learnt to exploit this excellent insulating material as a winter roosting place. Almost every Wellingtonia one examines will carry small scooped-out hollows in the bark with a line of white droppings beneath.

After the tree belt the way becomes more open again, and birds which might be seen in the sky here include Jackdaw, Carrion Crow, Rook, Lapwing and Heron. On the right the field boundary is an old dry-stone wall surmounted by a low hedge and this provides another habitat for animals and plants. (Try to identify mosses and ferns.) Here are some canes of Wild Raspberry, Pignut, White Dead-nettle and Meadow Saxifrage, while a damp area in the field opposite the Piggeries supports a fine patch of Cuckooflower or Lady's Smock.

Follow the road as it now runs to the right and passes Malleny Gardens which are owned and managed by the National Trust for Scotland. There is plenty of bird song to be heard in early summer as both cover and food are plentiful with woods, shrubberies, open lawns, farm buildings, hedges, fields and running water all available. In addition to birds already mentioned, look for Spotted Flycatcher, Pied Wagtail, Wren and any of the Warblers. The shrub border before the path rejoins Bridge Road, Balerno, contains a number of introduced garden species — Philadelphus, Maple species and Mahonia.

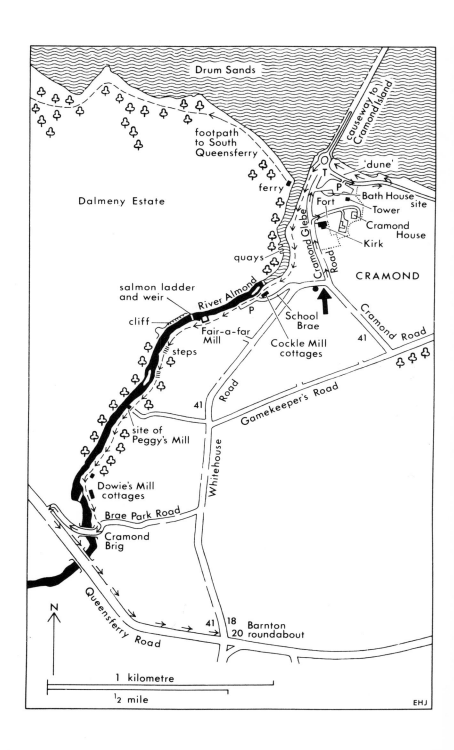

Drum Sands

footpath
to South
Queensferry

ferry

Dalmeny Estate

quays

salmon ladder
and weir

River Almond

cliff

Fair-a-far
Mill

steps

site of
Peggy's Mill

Dowie's Mill
cottages

Brae Park Road

Cramond
Brig

Causeway to Cramond Island

'dune'

T

P

Bath House
site

Fort

Tower

Cramond
House

Kirk

CRAMOND

Cramond Glebe Road

P

School
Brae

Cockle Mill
cottages

Cramond Road

41

Gamekeeper's Road

Whitehouse Road

41

Queensferry Road

41   18   Barnton
      20   roundabout

N

1 kilometre

½ mile

EHJ

Walk 6: The shore at Cramond and along the wooded valley of the River Almond

Starting Point   This walk begins at Cramond car park on the right at the bottom of Cramond Glebe Road. To reach it by public transport take either the 18 or 41 bus from Charlotte Square and descend at Cramond village. (On the map the walk starts at this point.)

At Cramond above the natural harbour at the mouth of the River Almond the Romans built a fort which they occupied from AD 140 for over 70 years. Archaeological investigations of a Bath House have been carried out on the land adjoining the car park, and before starting on the walk you may like to look at the excavations of the fort in the church grounds, a short distance up the road from the car park.

Distance   3 miles (4.8 km)

Walk down the promenade and turn right towards the east. If the tide is low many waders should be seen feeding on the wet sand, Dunlins, black and white Oystercatchers, flocks of hunch-backed Knots and graceful Redshanks are common, as are several of the gull family, Greater and Lesser Black-backed, Herring and Black-headed; Arctic Terns, Turnstones, Ringed Plovers and Curlew are frequently seen; the only common ducks here are Mallards, the male with its bottle-green head in the breeding season, and the black and white Shelduck with its brown band across the white. Bar-tailed Godwits can be occasionally sighted, most usually in winter. Any gathering of birds is worth careful scrutiny through binoculars for rarities.

Waders feed at the edge of the tide, probing in the sand or mud with beaks developed by evolution through the ages to facilitate this scavenging for shellfish, small crabs and worms. Their leavings in the form of broken shells dropped on the promenade from a height so that the bird can extract the edible part are readily observed. Oystercatchers are misnamed. They do not feed upon oysters but around the tide's edge like other waders. Dunlins, probably the commonest small wader, can be recognised in the breeding season by the black patch on the chest, and Knots are more stockily built than other waders.

Terns can be observed in summer. They are similar to, but more slender than, gulls and dive straight into the sea for fish, recalling their old name of sea-swallow. (The much bigger Gannet does the same.) The Common, Arctic and Sandwich Terns are difficult to distinguish in flight.

After about 330 yards (300 m) turn left down a few steps onto the beach. Before turning westward to retrace your steps along the shore line, look eastward for the raised beach, at the top of the field on the right, and seen even more conspicuously beyond the trees below the road (which stands out clearly when cars are on it), running along the summit of the grassy patch less than half a mile (1 km) distant. This is part of the raised beach against which ancient seas broke and dates from about 11,000 BC at the time of the last Ice Age when glaciers reached as far east as Stirling. It is roughly 50 feet (15 m) above Ordnance Datum, which is approximately mean sea level. The water has not retreated that distance in full in the last 13,000 years. Part of the change in level has been brought about by the elevation of the earth's surface when relieved of the weight of the ice cover as it melted (see Figure 16).

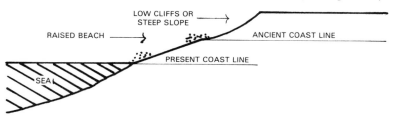

Figure 16: Section through a raised beach

On the beach at this point may be seen boulders of the two main rocks, the pale brown calciferous sandstone of the lower oil shale group and the dark grey volcanic rock, teschenite, a form of dolerite (an igneous rock coarser in grain than basalt). There are some small seaweed plants attached to them but these can be studied better along the causeway and on Cramond Island (see pages 35-9).

Walking westward towards the causeway to Cramond Island, the opportunity should be taken to search among the shells along the steepest part of the beach (see pages 35-9). Rocks in the intertidal zone, usually teschenite, are frequently barnacle-covered and small mussels abound. Probably because of the causeway accretion a reclamation of the land is taking place fairly quickly, 100 yards (100 m) or more in places, since the building of the promenade must have followed the coastline at the time of its construction in the late 1930s.

This stretch of sand is closest to a dune habitat within the confines of Edinburgh. Notice that the wide range of slightly raised sand parellel to the shore has been formed by Sea Lyme-grass with its bluish rigid leaves and stout underground stems spreading through the sand. The Sand Couch-grass with stiff pointed overground runners, grows beside the Lyme-grass in places. (Marram-grass, the commonest dune-forming grass is not evident on Cramond Beach.)

Amongst the loose sand and shingle there are salt resistant plants such as Sea Rocket, an annual which is scattered and widespread, and Sea Sandwort, a perennial which has crept over much of the sand. Both these plants have thick fleshy leaves. On the landward side of the 'dune' Coltsfoot, a plant of disturbed ground has spread widely and there are many fine plants of Mugwort, a common invader of waste places.

Some of the islands of the Forth which have been formed by intrusive igneous rocks (see pages 8-9) can be seen from the shore at Cramond. These include the close-in Cramond Island, already mentioned and not an island at low tide; Inchcolm island (part of Fife) with its Abbey which can be made out with field glasses, to the north; Inchmickery, mid-way between Inchcolm and Cramond Island, and the fortified island of Inchkeith (also part of Fife) to the north-east about three miles (nearly 5 km) north of Leith.

Beyond the causeway to Cramond Island the estuary of the River Almond, a river 28 miles (45 km) from its source near Kirk o' Shotts to its mouth and draining more than 65 square miles (168 square km) of West Lothian, is reached. First impression of water pollution may not be favourable but improvement has occurred in the last decade and migratory Salmon and Sea Trout penetrate each year in October or November to the point, near Livingston, where physical obstacles prevent further migration. Half a mile (1 km) upstream where the high weir is reached at Fair-a-Far (see map) a large fish ladder to facilitate fish movement has been constructed on the further bank of the Almond from the footpath.

Before leaving the estuary a further search for birds on the closest part of Drum Sands beyond the river should be made if the tide is low.

The walk continues past the houses of Cramond old village and the Boat Club house up the right bank of the river to Old Cramond Brig, about 1 mile (1.6 km) away. About 220 yards (200 m) beyond the boathouse the remains of three stone-built quays can be observed on the far bank, used by coastal shipping waiting to load or discharge cargoes 150 to 200 years ago when this river had a thriving, although small, ironworks industry. There were three mills — Cockle Mill, Fair-a-Far Mill and Dowie's Mill — for the production of nails, rod iron, spades and similar iron products between the mouth of the river and Cramond Old Brig and the remains of their workings, weirs and lades will be observed as the walk continues. Their productive history spans the years from 1750 to 1830. The fourth mill, Peggy's Mill, a little more than half way along the riverside part of the walk, produced paper.

The walk provides for much of its length a typical woodland habitat with adjacent running water. The native deciduous trees, Oak, Ash and Elm, have had added to them Lime, Horse Chestnut and Sycamore. The shrub layer includes regenerating trees, and Yew trees and Rhododendron bushes which have been planted. The herbaceous plants encountered are those typical of shady places, Wood Avens (Herb Bennet), Herb Robert and Dog's Mercury being particularly common. The flower of Wood Avens or Herb Bennet produces a head of hooked fruits which become attached to the fur or feathers of passing mammals and birds and become carried along probably to fall off some distance away where germination may take place.

Opposite the fenced-in boat enclosure on the side of the path away from the water there is a bank of Pick-a-back Plant (*Tolmiea menziesii*) with yellowish heart-shaped leaves and greenish flowers tinged with purple, a plant introduced into gardens from western North America and now naturalised in policies.

Just before the second car park at the foot of the brae known as School Brae notice that the Mill cottages of Cockle Mill have been restored.

Opposite School Brae is a small island where Mute Swans nest most springs and one or two cygnets are hatched. In 1977 the brood boasted seven young, all of which were successfully reared. Their progress up and down river, in convoy, rigorously escorted by their proud parents was a never to be forgotten sight for those lucky enough to see it.

Bird life on this stretch of river and woodland is varied. Dippers and Grey Wagtail should be looked for, along with Coot, Moorhen and Mallard; while Goldcrest are heard, more often than seen, near the tops of the smaller trees, below the weir at Fair-a-Far Mill already mentioned. Herons can be seen over-flying the river, while the Garden Warbler, almost extinct from this part twenty years ago, has returned in large enough numbers not to be a rarity. Just occasionally a Night Heron, a temporary escape from the Edinburgh Zoo, can be observed standing hunch-shouldered on the far bank scanning the water for fish. Treecreeper, Spotted Flycatcher and Blackcaps have been noted.

When the island at Cockle Mill has been passed, several exposed sections of the calciferous sandstone on the left of the path may be examined for varying angles of dip, indicative of severe earth folding and the non-conformities of the more recent sedimentary rocks with the older rock upon which they were deposited. Red stains of iron in the rocks can be seen in places. Much of the bedrock is overlain with boulder clay deposited at the time of the last Ice Age.

On the steep, often rocky sides of the valley grow many mosses, liverworts, lichens and ferns. The rocky area opposite the ruin of Fair-a-Far Mill is particularly rich in these. The Brittle Bladder Fern, a fern typical of moist rocky places, grows here as well as on the inside wall of the old mill; notice how some tree roots have penetrated into the cracks in the rocks. There is another very fine patch of Pick-a-back plant at the bottom of the rocky cliff.

Look towards the far side of the weir where the salmon ladder, already mentioned, may be seen. Also from June to September notice in the swamp and marshy zone of the far bank of the river below the weir the bright yellow flowers of Monkey-flower, a native of North America first recorded in this country in 1830 and now common on the edge of streams. Honeysuckle grows on the drier part of the bank above.

Above the weir the opposite bank of the river becomes a vertical cliff to which trees, Ivy and other plants are clinging. Close to the water's edge on this side Russian Comfrey, another naturalised plant, can be observed. Further upstream a gorge is reached.

Progress is facilitated by two flights of steps (one up, one down) as the original path over soft rock crumbled away some years ago. Notice the erosion of rocks by tree roots at the top of the first flight of steps. Continuing along the woodland path and down the second flight of steps it will be noted that nearly all the trees, mainly Beech, Wych Elm and Ash are past their prime, a great many on both banks having branches or even main trunks broken off. In certain areas regeneration is going on and there is a programme of replanting well under way.

The river is particularly attractive here, the water usually appearing fresh and sparkling. Reed Canary Grass edges the near bank in places and many bushes and trees of White Willow grow on the opposite bank. They become more numerous and taller, some over 60 feet (18 m) high, as the old Brig is approached.

The undergrowth of the woodland is rich in interesting herbaceous plants. In addition to those mentioned earlier in this account, they include Sweet Cicely, an Umbellifer, with its whitish flecked leaves and aroma of aniseed when crushed in the hand; Ramsons, a carpeting perennial resembling Lily-of-the-valley, smelling strongly of garlic in spring and early summer; Golden Saxifrage, a spring-flowering plant of stream sides and wet woods, and Great Woodrush growing in distinctive tussocks and usually found on rocky ground near streams. Further up the river, Butterbur, with the appearance of wild rhubarb, grows in rich profusion and beyond the low weir, from the same Daisy family, the small button-like yellow flowers of Tansy can be found. The earth beneath the trees is largely ivy-covered with leaves as veined and variegated as a garden variety, although the ivy carpet was established long before the gardens above the steep river banks began to be cultivated.

The Ink Cap fungus, also known as 'Lawyer's Wig' for reasons which will be obvious when it has been found, grows in clusters nearby at the side of the path.

Near the cottages of Dowie's Mill the walk continues past the low weir badly damaged by flood between the wars. Soon the old Cramond Brig, constructed in 1619, comes into sight. It was used as the main route between Edinburgh and Queensferry and hence the road to the north until the 1930s.

Turn right across the Brig, noting the inscriptions on the stones of the upstream face of the parapet, relating that it was 'repaired by both shires' (Linlithgowshire and Edinburghshire—to give them their old, then current, names) in 1687, 1761 'and again in 1776' and 1854. A glance along the outside upstream face of the bridge from the southern parapet will show the irregular stonework indicating the amount of settling of the bridge piers over almost four centuries.

On the outside downstream face of the bridge will be seen plants of Ivy-leaved Toadflax which have managed to find rootholds in the crevices between the stones. The flower stalks bend towards these cracks in the walls as the fruit ripens and when the fruit bursts the seeds become lodged in the cracks.

After pausing for a last look at the duck and waterfowl cross the bridge keeping Cramond Brig Hotel on the left and then turn left on to the trunk road to complete the walk. Public transport returning to Edinburgh can be picked up by walking back along the Edinburgh road to the Barnton roundabout, a distance of about a third of a mile (half a kilometre).

Suggestions for additional walks or visits

Six walks were chosen to cover examples of habitats within the Edinburgh boundary. The list below gives suggestions for further places to visit with much natural history interest.

Braid Hills Walk

Starting Point   Main Gate of Braid Hills Golf Course.

Distance   approximately 2½ miles (4 km). Allow plenty of time as much of the way is rough.

Buses 11 or 15 from town to Braid Hills Road. Walk up this road, crossing over Braid Road and bearing to the right along Braid Hills Approach. Walk through the Main Gate of the Golf Club and turn sharp left on to the bridle path. Follow this path right round the perimeter of the Golf Course. After descending the steep hill at the end of the walk, turn sharp right and skirt the back of the houses at Bramdean Rise, ending at Golf Course Car Park, and thence to Braid Hills Approach. Alternatively — Buses 18, 20, 31 or 37 to the top of Liberton Brae. Then walk along Liberton Drive until a *Gate* is reached on the left, opposite the Tower Kennels (just after the 30 mph sign). This leads on to the bridle path — see above.

   As the route described does not cross the Golf Course, it may be followed at any time; but if one wishes to diverge from the bridle path onto the course, it is preferable to take the walk on a Sunday, when there is no golf.

The Panorama

On a clear day, this walk affords a magnificent panoramic view of the Edinburgh area and beyond. From the Braid Hills — over 600 feet (183 metres) above sea level — the rocky nature of the local landscape, as described in the notes in the Introduction, is clearly seen in the many eminences, from west to east (those printed in italics are marked on Map 1 and/or Map 2) *Dalmahoy Hill*;

Craiglockhart Hill, with the Royal Edinburgh Hospital on its slopes; *Corstorphine Hill*, on the site of the Scottish Zoological Park; Edinburgh Castle Rock; Calton Hill with the Nelson Column, National Monument and City Observatory; Blackford Hill (see 2 on Map 2), with the Royal Observatory and Police Wireless Station; *Arthur's Seat*; *North Berwick Law*; the Garleton Hills, with Hopetoun Monument; and *Traprain Law*.

North of the City are the shining waters of the *Firth of Forth*, studded with little islands — Inchmickery, *Inchcolm, Inchkeith*, and the more distant *May Island* and *Bass Rock*, all of which may be seen when visibility is good, from various points along the walk.

Beyond the Forth, and to the west and north, one may catch sight of the far distant peak of Ben Lomond, and perhaps the Cobbler, the blue mountains of the Trossachs, the nearer *Ochil Hills*, the Bishop Hill, the *West* and *East Lomonds* and Largo Law.

Turning to the east and south, we see the rolling slopes of the *Lammermuirs* and *Moorfoot Hills*, followed by the *Pentlands*, ranging from *Caerketton* in the east to Bonaly and Torphin Hill in the west, with the tiny village of *Swanston* nestling in the foothills near the T-Wood (see walk No. 3).

Natural History

On the slopes of the Braids, on a summer day, one might expect to see such common birds as the Skylark, Blue Tit, Wren, Blackbird, Robin, Dunnock, Meadow Pipit, Linnet, Chaffinch and Yellow Hammer, while hirundines, such as Swift and Swallow, circle overhead in search of insects.

In the colder weather in autumn and winter, there might be flocks of finches, Lapwing, Common Gull, Wood Pigeon, Rook and Fieldfare foraging for food in the adjoining fields.

Unfortunately, it is too often found that fires — whether started accidentally or deliberately — tend to destroy some plant life on parts of the Braid Hills annually, but a list of the commoner plants still in evidence on the golf course side of the path after one such fire included the shrubs Bramble, Whin (Gorse), Elder and Hawthorn and herbaceous plants, typical of grassy places, such as Harebell (Scottish Bluebell), Wood Sage and Yarrow. Away from the bridle path look out for lime-loving grasses (see page 00).

There are several different species of trees which have been planted, between the path and the road.

Cammo Park and Beyond

On 25 April, 1980 the feu of Cammo Estate, once the property of Percival Maitland-Tennant and bequeathed by him to the National Trust for Scotland, was delivered by the Earl of Wemyss and March, President of the Trust, to Edinburgh's Lord Provost. Renamed Cammo Park, it now belongs to the Lothian Regional Council and is accessible to the public.

Starting Point   Main Gate of the Estate in Cammo Road. Buses 18, 20 and 41 to the bus terminus at Barnton roundabout, then a walk of ½ mile (0.8 km) along Cammo Road.

Alternatively, Bus 31 to the junction of Craigs Road and Maybury Road, then a walk of a little over half a mile (1 km) along Cammo Walk, a pleasant lane through open fields. The Park lies directly ahead and can be entered by taking a footpath left where the road turns sharply right. Although the whole area of the Park is relatively small, an hour or more can be spent exploring its numerous secluded paths.

The area comprises 104 acres (42 ha) of mature woodland and rough grassland which, through neglect over a number of years, has reverted to a state which justifies its epithet of 'Wilderness Park.' As such, it is unique among Edinburgh's many other more formal open spaces, since the intention is to leave its natural growth unchecked and so encourage wild life of all kinds to flourish.

Cammo House, once a large mansion of 52 rooms on three floors, was built in 1693 and is commonly believed to be the original of the House of Shaws so graphically described in the early chapters of R. L. Stevenson's *Kidnapped*. All that now remains of the building is a small part of the facade, but from the front door, raised as it is on a mound, the avenue planted by Sir John Clerk of Penicuik in 1710 can still be made out, with its long vista to the Pentland Hills. The stable block on the east of the estate, though roofless, is still quite well preserved and adjoining this is the old walled garden now wholly overgrown by a variety of plants which attract insects including many butterflies, and seed eating birds such as Chaffinch, Greenfinch and Goldfinch. There is a rookery near the main gate and other birds regularly seen include Wren, Dunnock and Coal Tit. Fieldfare, Redwing and Curlew are often to be seen on the grassland in winter months. Badgers, Foxes, Rabbits and Grey Squirrels inhabit the woodland, which consists of fine mature trees, mainly Beech, Pedunculate Oak, Yew and Sweet Chestnut. There is a rich variety of fungi, particularly on the many decaying branches and tree stumps. Behind the house is a long pond draining into an old narrow canal and there are large colourful species of Rhododendron nearby.

A visit to the Park can be extended by following Cammo Road beyond the main entrance. Continue until the very last house has been reached, past which a footpath on the right follows the River Almond upstream, ending at the railway line close to Turnhouse Airport. A track to the left follows the railway line to rejoin Cammo Road making a circular walk of some two miles, just over three kilometres, from the Park.

Alternatively the River may be crossed by an old bridge a little along the footpath, from which the route goes downstream on the left bank to Cramond Brig Hotel, joining the end of Walk 6 — a distance of 1 mile (1.6 km).

The paths are wooded for much of the way and plants such as Butterbur, Lungwort, Few-flowered Leek, Ramsons, Leopard's-bane and Giant Bellflower may be seen at the riverside.

Corstorphine Hill

To a greater extent than any other of the hills of Edinburgh, Corstorphine Hill is a woodland area, and under the cover of such vegetation a wealth of wildlife has been able to survive here despite human pressure from the housing estates, the Zoological Park and the golf courses which surround this Public Park.

Access Points   The main access points to the maze of footpaths are — in the south, from Corstorphine Road opposite Balgreen Road and from the top of Kaimes Road (Bus Nos. 12, 26, 31); on the west, three points in Clermiston Road (Bus Nos, 26, 86); from Queensferry Road (Bus No. 18); and from Craigcrook Road and Ravelston Dykes Road, on the east (Bus Nos. 13, 38); and there is a (one-way!) revolving gate in the north fence of the Zoological Park.

Corstorphine Hill was created by the intrusion of volcanic rocks into the sedimentary deposits (see page 11 and Figure 1), when the whole of this area was a shallow sea. This volcanic sill was slowly exposed by erosion through the centuries, and the smooth bare slabs of rock which are a feature of several places on the hill are glaciated pavements formed during the last Ice Age some 12,000 years ago. The present-day height of the hill is 530 feet (162 metres) surmounted by the 70 feet (21 metres) of the Clermiston Tower built in 1851, the centenary of Sir Walter Scott's birth. Over the centuries the whole district has been drying out, and even in recent years the natural water supply has been decreasing steadily, with drainage on the lower fields and infilling of quarries, and this factor may in years to come affect the habitats and wildlife of the Hill.

The greater part of the woodlands today consists of broad-leaved trees, many of them introduced in recent times. There are good stands of Beech, in the shade of which there is little or no ground cover; Sycamore, Elm, Lime Ash, Horse Chestnut, and both Sessile and Pedunculate Oak, while smaller species are Birch, Rowan, Hazel, Hawthorn and Holly. Confers are represented by some Scots Pine, Larch, Norway Spruce and a few Yew. Rhododendron thickets, Brambles, Wild Raspberries, Ivy, Wild Rose and Gorse (Whin) provide essential cover for wildlife as well as adding their own beauty. Botanically, there are few rarities left on the Hill; human pressure has eliminated the primroses and reduced the wild hyacinths, but a good selection of common woodland and heathland plants thrive in the widely assorted habitats available, from the dry sunny grassland of south-facing slopes, through rocky crevices, quarries, birch-groves, hawthorn scrub, to deep woodland.

The mammal population of the Hill is far greater than that seen by a day-time visitor, as most species are nocturnal, and the grey squirrel is the only one likely to be encountered, but a walk after a night's snowfall will disclose a surprising network of footprints! Badgers are here in good numbers and though the setts are often well-concealed in gorse or bramble thickets, there is an old established and easily-found sett, in the trees on the right of the path, about 100 yards (133 metres) north of Clermiston Tower. It is not unknown for both badgers and foxes to be seen at dusk scavenging in suburban gardens nearby. Mole-hills and rabbit-burrows can be readily seen, but smaller mammals such as bank vole and field vole, shrew and wood mouse are likely to go undetected.

The varied habitats on Corstorphine Hill attract a very good number of birds, the figure for a survey in 1976 being 58 species, but this of course included summer and winter visitors and others merely 'passing through' on the way to other areas. The residents are the comparatively common birds such as Blackbird, Dunnock, Robin, Chaffinch, Greenfinch, Blue Tit and Great Tit, Wren, Woodpigeon, Song Thrush, Mistle Thrush and Carrion Crow, but also regularly seen are Magpie, Jackdaw, Treecreeper, Green Woodpecker and Great Spotted Woodpecker, Tree Sparrow and Linnet. The birdsongs of early summer include those of the Willow Warbler, Wood Warbler, Whitethroat and Blackcap, while winter brings small foraging flocks of Redwing, Fieldfare and Brambling.

At any time of year, an excursion to Corstorphine Hill can offer attractive 'country walks' over very varied terrain and excellent views of Edinburgh and the surrounding countryside to all points of the compass.

Leith Docks and Seafield

See page 40, and list of Seabirds and Waders on page 120.

Royal Botanic Garden

Outstanding botanical interest with a rich collection of trees and shrubs, and rock, woodland and peat gardens. Readers are referred to the booklet, *The Garden Companion*, which can be purchased at the Main Entrance to the Garden.

Animals to be seen within the Garden include some birds, even Kingfisher and Water Rail, not often seen within the City boundary, squirrels, foxes and frogs.

Water of Leith Walkway

The Walkway beside the Water of Leith which was developed in the 1970s by the City Planning Department of Edinburgh Corporation, later to become the City of Edinburgh District Council, runs from Balerno to Slateford, a distance of 5½ miles (8.4 km). It is hoped that it will eventually run the whole distance from the Pentlands to the Forth. Two new short sections have recently been added. One, the Dean Bank Footpath, opened in 1977, runs on the left bank of the Water of Leith from Belford Bridge to Dean Path and the second, the Deanhaugh Footpath from Stockbridge to Falshaw Bridge, a distance of a little more than a quarter of a mile.

Information pamphlets giving features of historical and archaeological interest as well as natural history of the Walkway and the two new Footpaths may be obtained free of charge from the City Planning Department, 3 Market Street. There is a very interesting exhibition of photographs of the Water of Leith and proposed plans for its development in Cockburn Street, next to the Planning Department.

The part of the Walkway from Balerno to Currie has been included in Walk 5. The stretch from Currie to Slateford also provides a variety of interesting habitats. A suggested walk on this stretch is upstream from Slateford to Colinton (1½ miles – 2.3 km) and on to Juniper Green, a further 1½ miles (2.3 km).

Starting Point — The path beside the Dell Inn on the Lanark Road, Slateford. Bus 44 — there is a bus stop not far from the beginning of the path.

Before leaving the Lanark Road notice the weir on the Water of Leith just before it runs under the road. On the other side of the road there is the high aqueduct of the Union Canal with its overspill passing into the Water below.

The first part of the walk (not part of the official Walkway) passes through the mixed woodland of Craiglockhart Dell with trees planted in the late 1700s. Grottoes must have been put up at the same time. Woodland herbaceous plants not far from the track include Ramsons, Dog's Mercury, Wood Sanicle and Wood Avens. In the deep shade Ivy covers the ground. Introduced plants, now naturalised, include Fringe Cups (*Tellima grandiflora*) a close relative of the Pick-a-back plant found in the woods at Cramond — and the shrub Fly Honeysuckle. On either side of the track at the entrance to the woodland there are plants typical of disturbed and waste ground including Coltsfoot, Hairy Bittercress, Shepherd's Purse and Groundsel.

A set of wooden steps leads down from the Dell to a path crossing a grassy area to the Water. Notice a very fine Hornbeam tree at the stone bridge over the Water. Cross this Bridge and continue straight forward on the path for a short distance until you pass under the old railway bridge. Immediately climb up steps on the left to get on to the railway track. You are now on the official Walkway which starts at the footbridge over the Lanark Road near the Canal.

Continue westward along the railway track with its lining of bushy trees — mostly of Elder and Elm — and typical herbaceous plants growing in their shade.

Along the course followed by the walk over 80 species of birds have been identified. It is very easy to sidetrack from the railway path on to one of the smaller paths down the side of the Dell to the Water where you may see a Dipper, a small bird which is dark brown with a white breast. It often stands on rocks in the water bobbing and dipping its head and feeding on water animals such as insect nymphs, water beetles, caddis larvae or small fish. You may also see the Pied Wagtail, with its grey and white plumage and the Grey Wagtail, grey in colour with black tail but with yellow chest.

Continuing on the main Walkway a stretch of path is reached where gardens come down to the path. Notice the trees which include Copper Beech, Spanish Chestnut and Atlantic Cedar, a conifer not noted on any of the six walks.

Soon a stretch of the pathway is reached where on the right of the path there is a steep rocky slope of calciferous sandstone. As a result of clearance in the mid 1970s there are grassy areas — succession has been allowed to go on since then so they are becoming scrubby — where grow lime-loving plants such as Crosswort, Sweet Woodruff and Burnet Saxifrage; further on where the slope is overhung by a canopy of trees, are ferns such as Hart's-tongue, Lady-fern and Hard Shield-fern (Prickly Shield-fern) which like limy shady situations. They are not widespread in the Edinburgh District.

From this wooded area you may leave the Walkway taking the sign-posted path to the left down the steep slope of Colinton Dell and along the path at the side of the Water, then on past Colinton Church into the village for a bus back to town. There are many fine trees in Colinton Dell and near the path past the Church, as well as ferns and a rich collection of mosses, liverworts and lichens.

If you continue along the Walkway you pass through a tunnel 160 yards (156 metres) long to the area where once was Colinton station and which has now been landscaped. Passing the gate in Spylaw Park the Walkway continues to Juniper Green. Most of the way is well wooded with the Ash, a tree which flourishes on lime-rich soil, much in evidence. The south-facing slope from the Lanark Road down to the Water on the far side provides ideal growing conditions for the market gardens which have developed there.

You may continue on the Walkway from Juniper Green to Currie linking up with the Currie to Balerno stretch covered in Walk No. 5.

Cemeteries

Cemeteries and burial grounds provide habitats for a range of wildlife and are especially valuable when located in built-up areas of the city.

Many of the private cemeteries have unfortunately suffered from neglect and lack of regular maintenance in recent years; however, their semi-natural state has enhanced their natural history value, for example, in Warriston cemetery, which fringes the Water of Leith.

Edinburgh District Council would hope to acquire these cemeteries, at some time in the future. It is intended that they would be maintained, in a semi-natural state, and managed in a manner which would respect their existing and potential natural history value.

Plants and animals

Below are lists of plants and animals which have been seen or, in the case of animals, noted indirectly by members of the Edinburgh Natural History Society on the walks described or at some places mentioned in the introduction.

It must be emphasised that they do not set out to give comprehensive lists of the *whole* area and species seen will vary with the time of year. In the columns at the side of the lists, walkers may record their own observations and spaces are provided for entries of additional species seen.

For ease of reference the plants and animals have been listed in alphabetical order of the English names. This has often proved difficult for plants, for so many of them have more than one English name in common use. The English names used are based on those in the list drawn up by the Botanical Society of the British Isles, though in some cases the alternative names have also been put in. The Latin names, which are standard throughout the world, follow.

Flowering Plants

These include non-woody or herbaceous plants, shrubs and trees

Herbaceous plants

(The list omits grasses, rushes and sedges.)

		Walk					
English name	Latin name	1	2	3	4	5	6
Agrimony	*Agrimonia eupatoria*						
Anemone, Wood	*Anemone nemorosa*						
Angelica, Wild	*Angelica sylvestris*						
Archangel, Yellow	*Lamiastrum galeobdolon*						
Avens, Water	*Geum rivale*						
Avens, Wood (Herb Bennet)	*Geum urbanum*						
Avens, Hybrid	*G. rivale x urbanum*						

		Walk					
English name	**Latin name**	**1**	**2**	**3**	**4**	**5**	**6**
Balsam, Indian (Policeman's Helmet)	*Impatiens glandulifera*						
Basil, Wild	*Clinopodium vulgare*						
Bedstraw, Heath	*Galium saxatile*						
Hedge	*mollugo*						
Lady's	*verum*						
Bindweed, Field	*Convolvulus arvensis*						
Hedge	*Calystegia sepium*						
Bird's-foot-trefoil	*Lotus corniculatus*						
Bistort, Common	*Polygonum bistorta*						
Bitter-cress, Hairy	*Cardamine hirsuta*						
Large	*amara*						
Wavy	*flexuosa*						
Blood-drop-emlets	*Mimulus luteus*						
Bluebell (Wild Hyacinth)	*Endymion non-scriptus*						
Brooklime	*Veronica beccabunga*						
Bugle	*Ajuga reptans*						
Burdock, Greater	*Arctium lappa*						
Lesser	*minus*						
Butterbur	*Petasites hybridus*						
Giant	*japonicus*						
Buttercup, Bulbous	*Ranunculus bulbosus*						
Creeping	*repens*						
Meadow	*acris*						
Campion, Bladder	*Silene vulgaris*						
Red	*dioica*						
Cat's-ear, Common	*Hypochoeris radicata*						
Celandine, Lesser	*Ranunculus ficaria*						
Charlock	*Sinapsis arvensis*						
Chervil, Rough	*Chaerophyllum temulentum*						
Chickweed, Common	*Stellaria media*						
Cicely, Sweet	*Myrrhis odorata*						
Cinquefoil, Creeping	*Potentilla reptans*						
Marsh	*palustris*						
Cleavers (Goosegrass or Sticky Willie)	*Galium aparine*						
Clover, Red	*Trifolium pratense*						
White	*repens*						
Zig Zag	*medium*						
Coltsfoot	*Tussilago farfara*						
Comfrey, Common	*Symphytum officinale*						
Russian	*x uplandicum*						
Tuberous	*tuberosum*						
Cranesbill, Bloody	*Geranium sangluneum*						
Dove's-foot	*molle*						
Hedgerow	*pyrenaicum*						
Meadow	*pratense*						
Wood	*sylvaticum*						
Crosswort	*Cruciata laevipes (Galium cruciata)*						
Crowfoot, Common Water	*Ranunculus aquatillis*						
Cuckooflower (Lady's Smock)	*Cardamine pratensis*						

Walk

English name	Latin name	1	2	3	4	5	6
Daisy	*Bellis perennis*						
Daisy, Ox-eye	*Leucanthemum vulgare*						
Dame's Violet	*Hesperis matronalis*						
Dandelion	*Taraxacum officinale*						
Dead-nettle, Cut-leaved	*Lamium hybridum*						
Red	*purpureum*						
Spotted	*maculatum*						
White	*album*						
Dock, Broad-leaved	*Rumex obtusifolius*						
Curled	*crispus*						
Wood	*sanguineus*						
Dog's Mercury	*Mercurialis perennis*						
Duckweed, Common	*Lemna minor*						
Fat	*gibba*						
Ivy-leaved	*trisulca*						
Enchanter's Nightshade	*Circaea lutetiana*						
Eyebright	*Euphrasia officinalis*						
Fat-hen	*Chenopodium album*						
Feverfew	*Tanacetum parthenium*						
Figwort, Common	*Schrophularia nodosa*						
Forget-me-not, Changing	*Myosotis discolor*						
Early	*ramosissima*						
Field	*arvensis*						
Tufted	*caespitosa*						
Water	*scorpioides*						
Wood	*sylvatica*						
Foxglove	*Digitalis purpurea*						
Fumitory, Common	*Fumaria officinalis*						
Garlic, Field	*Allium oleraceum*						
Garlic Mustard (Jack-by-the-Hedge)	*Alliaria petiolata*						
Golden Saxifrage, Opposite-leaved	*Chrysosplenium oppositifolium*						
Ground Elder (Bishop's Weed)	*Aegopodium podagraria*						
Ground Ivy	*Glechoma hederacea*						
Groundsel	*Senecio vulgaris*						
Sticky	*viscosus*						
Harebell (Scottish Bluebell)	*Campanula rotundifolia*						
Hawk's-beard, Smooth	*Crepis capillaris*						
Hawkweed, Mouse-ear	*Hireacium pilosella*						
other spp.	*spp.*						
Hedge Mustard	*Sisymbrium officinale*						
Hedge-Parsley, Upright	*Torilis japonica*						
Hemlock	*Conium maculatum*						
Herb Robert	*Geranium robertianum*						
Hogweed	*Heracleum sphondylium*						
Hogweed, Giant	*mantegazzianum*						
Iris, Yellow	*Iris pseudacorus*						

English name	Latin name	Walk					
		1	2	3	4	5	6
Knapweed, Common (Hardheads)	*Centaurea nigra*						
Knotgrass	*Polygonum aviculare*						
Knotweed, Giant	*sachalinense*						
Japanese	*cuspidatum*						
Lady's Mantle	*Alchemilla vulgaris*						
Leek, Few-flowered	*Allium paradoxum*						
Leopard's-bane	*Doronicum pardalianches*						
London Pride	*Saxifraga spathularis x umbrosa*						
Mayweed, Scentless	*Tripleurospermum maritimum sub sp. inodorum*						
Meadowsweet	*Filipendula ulmaria*						
Medick, Black	*Medicago lupulina*						
Milkwort, Common	*Polygala vulgaris*						
Mint, Water	*Mentha aquatica*						
Monkeyflower	*Mimulus guttatus*						
Moschatel	*Adoxa moschatellina*						
Mouse-ear, Common (Chickweed)	*Cerastium holosteoides*						
Sticky	*glomeratum*						
Mugwort	*Artemesia vulgaris*						
Mullein, Great	*Verbascum thapsus*						
Nettle, Stinging	*Urtica dioica*						
Nipplewort	*Lapsana communis*						
Orache, Frosted	*Atriplex laciniata*						
Common	*patula*						
Orpine	*Sedum telephium*						
Parsley, Cow	*Anthriscus sylvestris*						
Pearlwort, Procumbent	*Sagina procumbens*						
Periwinkle, Lesser	*Vinca minor*						
Pick-a-back-plant	*Tolmiea menziesii*						
Pignut	*Conopodium majus*						
Pineappleweed	*Matricaria matricarioides*						
Plantain, Greater	*Plantago major*						
Ribwort	*lanceolata*						
Pondweed, Broad-leaved (Floating)	*Potamogeton natans*						
Poppy, Common	*Papaver rhoeas*						
Welsh	*Meconopsis cambrica*						
Primrose	*Primula vulgaris*						
Purslane, Pink	*Montia sibirica*						
Ragged Robin	*Lychnis flos-cuculi*						
Ragwort, Common	*Senecio jacobaea*						
Oxford	*squalidus*						
Ramsons	*Allium ursinum*						
Redshank (Persicaria)	*Polygonum persicaria*						
Restharrow	*Ononis repens*						

Walk

English name	Latin name	1	2	3	4	5	6
Rock-cress, Hairy	*Arabis hirsuta*						
Rocket, Sea	*Cakile maritima*						
Rock-rose, Common	*Helianthemum chamaecistus*						
St John's Wort, Square-stemmed	*Hypericum tetrapterum*						
Perforate	*perforatum*						
Beautiful	*pulchrum*						
Sage, Wood	*Teucrium scorodonia*						
Sandwort, Sea	*Honkenya peploides*						
Three-nerved	*Moehringia trinervia*						
Thyme-leaved	*Arenaria serpylifolia*						
Sanicle	*Sanicula europaea*						
Scabious, Devil's-bit	*Succisa pratensis*						
Field	*Knautia arvensis*						
Selfheal	*Prunella vulgaris*						
Shepherd's Purse	*Capsella bursa-pastoris*						
Silverweed	*Potentilla anserina*						
Sneezewort	*Achillea ptarmica*						
Snowdrop	*Galanthus nivalis*						
Solomon's Seal	*Polygonatum multiflorum*						
Sorrel, Common	*Rumex acetosa*						
Sheep's	*acetosella*						
Sow Thistle, Smooth	*Sonchus oleraceus*						
Speedwell, Common Field	*Veronica persica*						
Germander	*chamaedrys*						
Slender	*filiformis*						
Wall	*arvensis*						
Spurrey, Corn	*Spergula arvensis*						
Stitchwort, Greater	*Stellaria holostea*						
Lesser	*graminea*						
Stonecrop, Biting	*Sedum acre*						
Strawberry, Barren	*Potentilla sterilis*						
Wild	*Fragaria vesca*						
Tansy	*Tanacetum vulgare*						
Tare, Hairy	*Vicia hirsuta*						
Thistle, Creeping	*Cirsium arvense*						
Spear	*vulgare*						
Thyme	*Thymus drucei*						
Toadflax, Common	*Linaria vulgaris*						
Ivy-leaved	*Cymbalaria muralis*						
Purple	*Linaria purpurea*						
Tormentil	*Potentilla erecta*						
Trefoil, Hop	*Trifolium campestre*						
Lesser	*dubium*						
Valerian, Common	*Valeriana officinalis*						
Pyrenean	*pyrenaica*						
Vetch, Bush	*Vicia sepium*						
Common	*sativa*						
Tufted	*cracca*						
Vetchling, Meadow	*Lathyrus pratensis*						

Walk

English name	Latin name	1	2	3	4	5	6
Violet, Common Dog	*Viola riviniana*						
Viper's Bugloss	*Echium vulgare*						
Water-cress	*Rorippa nasturtium-aquaticum*						
Weld (Dyer's Rocket)	*Reseda luteola*						
Willowherb, Broad-leaved	*Epilobium montanum*						
Great	*hirsutum*						
Rosebay	*angustifolium*						
Woodruff	*Galium odoratum*						
Wood-sorrel	*Oxalis acetosella*						
Wormwood	*Artemisia absinthium*						
Woundwort, Hedge	*Stachys sylvatica*						
Yarrow	*Achillea millefolium*						

Other herbaceous plants seen:

Shrubs

Woody plants with several woody stems, branching near or from ground level

Walk

English name	Latin name	1	2	3	4	5	6
Barberry	*Berberis vulgaris*						
Bilberry (Blaeberry)	*Vaccinium myrtillus*						
Blackthorn	*Prunus spinosa*						
Bramble (Blackberry)	*Rubus fruticosus*						
Broom	*Sarothamnus scoparius*						
Buckthorn, Sea	*Hippophae rhamnoides*						

Walk

English name	Latin name	1	2	3	4	5	6
Buddleia (Butterfly Bush)	*Buddleia daxidii*						
Cotoneaster sp.	*Cotoneaster*						
Crowberry	*Empetrum nigrum*						
Currant, Flowering	*Ribes sanguineum*						
Dogwood	*Thelycrania sanguinea*						
Elder	*Sambucus nigra*						
Red-berried	*racemosa*						
Gooseberry	*Ribes uva-crispa*						
Gorse (Whin)	*Ulex europaeus*						
Hawthorn	*Crataegus monogyna*						
Heath, Cross-leaved	*Erica tetralix*						
Heather, Bell	*cinerea*						
Heather, Ling	*Calluna vulgarus*						
Honeysuckle	*Lonicera periclymenum*						
Ivy	*Hedera helix*						
Juniper	*Juniperus communis*						
Laurel, Cherry	*Prunus laurocerasus*						
Portugal	*lusitanica*						
Lilac	*Syringa vulgaris*						
Mahonia (Oregon Grape)	*Mahonia aquifolium*						
Mock Orange	*Philadelphus coronarius*						
Privet, Garden	*Ligustrum ovalifolium*						
Wild	*vulgare*						
Raspberry	*Rubus idaeus*						
Rhododendron	*Rhododendron ponticum*						
Rose, Dog	*Rosa canina*						
Downy	*villosa*						
Japanese	*rugosa*						
Snowberry	*Symphoricarpos rivularis*						
Willows (see tree list)							

Other Shrubs seen:

Trees

		Walk					
English name	**Latin name**	1	2	3	4	5	6

Broad-leaved trees

English name	Latin name
Alder	*Alnus glutinosa*
Ash	*Fraxinus excelsior*
Beech	*Fagus sylvatica*
Birch, Downy	*Betula pubescens*
Silver	*pendula*
Cherry, Bird	*Prunus padus*
Wild	*avium*
Chestnut, Horse	*Aesculus hippocastanum*
Sweet	*Castanea sativa*
Elm, English	*Ulmus procera*
Wych	*glabra*
Hazel	*Corylus avellana*
Holly	*Ilex aquifolium*
Hornbeam	*Carpinus betulus*
Laburnum	*Laburnum spp.*
Lime	*Tilia x vulgaris*
Maple, Field	*Acer campestre*
Norway	*platanoides*
Oak, Pedunculate	*Quercus robur*
Sessile	*petraea*
Turkey	*cerris*
Osier	*Salix viminalis*
Pear, Wild	*Pyrus communis*
Plum, Purple-leaved	*Prunus cerasifera*
	var. atropurpurea
Poplar, Black (hybrid)	*Populus nigra*
White	*alba*
Rowan (Mountain Ash)	*Sorbus aucuparia*
Sycamore	*Acer pseudoplatanus*
Walnut	*Juglans regia*
Whitebeam, Common	*Sorbus aria*
Swedish	*intermedia*
Willow, Crack	*Salix fragilis*
Goat (Great Sallow)	*caprea*
Grey (Common ,,)	*atrocinerea*
White	*alba*

Walk

English name	Latin name	1	2	3	4	5	6
Conifers							
Cedar, Western Red	*Thuja plicata*						
Cedar (true) of Lebanon	*Cedrus libani*						
Atlas	*atlantica*						
Cypress, Lawson	*Chamaecyparis lawsoniana*						
Leyland	*Cupressocyparis leylandii*						
Fir, Douglas	*Pseudotsuga menziesii*						
Hemlock, Western	*Tsuga heterophylla*						
Larch, European	*Larix decidua*						
Japanese	*kaempferi*						
Pine, Austrian	*Pinus nigra*						
Scots	*sylvestris*						
Spruce, Norway	*Picea abies*						
Sitka	*stitchensis*						
Wellingtonia	*Sequioadendron giganteum*						
Yew	*Taxus baccata*						

Other trees seen:

Flowerless Plants (These include ferns and horsetails, fungi, mosses and liverworts, lichens and seaweeds. Some have been mentioned in Part I or pointed out on the walks. For identification readers should refer to one of the books given on page 122).

Insects and Other Invertebrates

(animals without backbones)

There is ample scope for the study of insects and other invertebrates on the walks.

Insects

Examples within twelve of the main orders (groups) of insects which may be seen on the walks are given below (to help with tracing specimens in an identification book the names of the twelve orders are given).

Ephemeroptera	Mayflies
Odonata	Dragonflies and damselflies
Plecoptera	Stoneflies
Orthoptera	Grasshoppers and crickets
Dermaptera	Earwigs
Hemiptera (True Bugs)	Aphids, Water Scorpion, Water Boatman, Pond Skaters
Neuroptera	Alder flies
Lepidoptera	Butterflies and Moths
Trichoptera	Caddis flies
Diptera (True Flies)	House-fly, Crane-fly (Daddy-long-legs), Gnats, Midges, Mosquitoes, Hover-flies
Hymenoptera	Bees, Wasps, Ants, Saw-flies
Coleoptera	Beetles

(**Note:** an insect may be captured and placed in a small box with transparent lid for examination but it should be released as soon as possible.)

Invertebrates other than insects

Some of these have been mentioned in the text, e.g. earthworms, flatworms, leeches, lugworms, shell fish, water louse, but many more may be seen. For identification readers should refer to *The Oxford Book of Invertibrates.*

Reptiles and Amphibia

Reptiles

Although the Common Lizard (*Lacerta vivipara*) is to be found within the Edinburgh boundary it is unlikely that one will be seen on any of the walks or visits.

Amphibia

Look out for frogs, toads, and newts (and in spring, spawn) in or near fresh water, especially on Walk 4 along the side of the canal and Walk 5 along the Water of Leith. Over the last decades they have become far less common owing to loss of habitat, but the following have been seen in the Edinburgh area in recent years: Common Frog (*Rana temporaria*); Common Toad (*Bufo bufo*); Common Newt (*Triturus vulgaris*); Palmate Newt (*Triturus helveticus*) and on rare occasions Great Crested Newt (*Triturus cristatus*).

Mammals

Some mammals which live within the City boundary are occasionally seen on the walks or on visits to other parts of the City, but it is more likely that indirect evidence of their presence such as footprints, tree bark damage to saplings, a squirrel drey, a molehill, fox den or badger sett will be noted instead.

English name	Latin name	Sightings and/or signs
Badger	*Meles meles*	
Bat spp.[1]	*Myotis spp.* and *Pipistrellus spp.*	
Deer, Roe	*Capreolus capreolus*	
Fox	*Vulpes vulpes*	
Hare, Brown	*Lepus capensis*	
Mountain	*timidus*	
Hedgehog	*Erinaceus europeaus*	
Mink	*Mustela vison*	
Mole	*Talpa europaea*	
Mouse, House	*Mus musculus*	
Wood	*Apodemus sylvaticus*	
Rabbit	*Oryctolagus cuniculus*	
Rat, Common (Brown Rat)	*Rattus norvegicus*	
Seal, Common	*Phoca vitulina*	
Grey	*Halichoerus grypus*	
Shrew, Common[3]	*Sorex araneus*	
Pygmy	*minutus*	
Water	*Neomys fodiens*	
Stoat	*Mustela erminea*	
Squirrel, Grey	*Sciurus carolinensis*	
Vole, Bank	*Clethrionomys glareolus*	
Field	*Microtus agrestis*	
Water	*Arvicola terrestris*	
Weasel	*Mustela nivalis*	

Notes:

[1] It is difficult to distinguish species of bat while on the wing.

[2] Common Seals are often close in shore while the Grey Seal is a less frequent visitor.

[3] Shrew are very seldom seen although the Common Shrew may often be found dead on paths in the autumn.

Birds

About 200 species of birds have been recorded within the City but the sighting of some is unusual.

Below are lists of birds which members of the Society have seen or heard frequently (or which might possibly be seen) on Walks 2, 3, 5 and 6, and at Duddingston, and from Leith Docks and Seafield. Space is provided for recording sightings on different dates.

Walk 2 — Blackford Hill and Hermitage of Braid

English name	Latin name	Dates on which seen
Residents		
Blackbird	*Turdus merula*	
Bullfinch	*Pyrrhula pyrrhula*	
Chaffinch	*Fringilla coelebs*	
Coot	*Fulica atra*	
Crow, Carrion	*Corvus corone*	
Dipper	*Cinclus cinclus*	
Duck, Tufted	*Aythya fuligula*	
Dunnock	*Prunella modularis*	
Goldfinch	*Carduelis carduelis*	
Greenfinch	*Carduelis chloris*	
Gull, Black-headed	*Larus ridibundus*	
Common	*canus*	
Herring	*argentatus*	
Jackdaw	*Corvus monedula*	
Kestrel	*Falco tinnunculus*	
Linnet	*Carduelis cannabina*	
Magpie	*Pica pica*	
Mallard	*Anas platyrhynchos*	
Moorhen	*Gallinula chloropus*	
Pipit, Meadow	*Anthus pratensis*	

English name	Latin name	Dates on which seen
Robin	*Erithacus rubecula*	
Rook	*Corvus frugilegus*	
Skylark	*Alauda arvensis*	
Starling	*Sturnus vulgaris*	
Thrush, Mistle	*Turdus viscivorus*	
Song	*philomelos*	
Tit, Blue	*Parus caeruleus*	
Coal	*ater*	
Great	*major*	
Long-tailed	*Aegithalos caudatus*	
Treecreeper	*Certhia familiaris*	
Wagtail, Grey	*Motacilla cinerea*	
Pied	*alba*	
Woodpecker, Great Spotted	*Dendrocopos major*	
Green	*Picus viridis*	
Woodpigeon	*Columba palumbus*	
Wren	*Troglodytes troglodytes*	
Yellowhammer	*Emberiza citrinella*	

Summer visitors

Blackcap	*Sylvia atricapilla*	
Flycatcher, Spotted	*Muscicapa striata*	
Martin, House	*Delichon urbica*	
Swallow	*Hirundo rustica*	
Swift	*Apus apus*	
Warbler, Willow	*Phylloscopus trachilus*	
Whitethroat	*Sylvia communis*	

Winter visitors

Brambling	*Fringilla montifringilla*	
Redwing	*Turdus iliacus*	

Other birds seen

Walks 3a and 3b — Pentland Hill Walks

English name	Latin name	Dates on which seen
Residents		
Blackbird	*Turdus merula*	
Chaffinch	*Fringilla coelebs*	
Crow, Carrion	*Corvus corone*	
Curlew	*Numenius arquata*	
Dunnock	*Prunella modularis*	
Goldcrest	*Regulus regulus*	
Goldfinch	*Carduelis carduelis*	
Greenfinch	*Carduelis chloris*	
Grouse, Red	*Lagopus lagopus*	
Jackdaw	*Corvus monedula*	
Kestrel	*Falco tinnunculus*	
Lapwing	*Vanellus vanellus*	
Linnet	*Carduelis cannabina*	
Pipit, Meadow	*Anthus pratensis*	
Robin	*Erithacus rubecula*	
Rook	*Corvus frugilegus*	
Skylark	*Alauda arvensis*	
Sparrow, House	*Passer domesticus*	
Starling	*Sturnus vulgaris*	
Stonechat	*Saxicola torquata*	
Thrush, Mistle	*Turdus viscivorus*	
Song	*philomelos*	
Tit, Blue	*Parus caeruleus*	
Coal	*ater*	
Great	*major*	
Wagtail, Pied	*Motacilla alba*	
Woodpigeon	*Columba palumbus*	
Wren	*Troglodytes troglodytes*	
Yellowhammer	*Emberiza citrinella*	
Summer visitors		
Cuckoo	*Cuculus canorus*	
Martin, House	*Delichon urbica*	

English name	Latin name	Dates on which seen
Swallow	*Hirundo rustica*	
Swift	*Apus apus*	
Warbler, Willow	*Phylloscopus trochilus*	
Wheatear	*Oenanthe oenanthe*	
Whinchat	*Saxicola rubetra*	

Winter visitors

Brambling	*Fringilla montifringilla*	
Fieldfare	*Turdus pilaris*	
Redwing	*Turdus iliacus*	

Other birds seen

Walk 5 — Balerno — Currie

English name	Latin name	Dates on which seen
Residents		
Blackbird	*Turdus merula*	
Bullfinch	*Pyrrhula pyrrhula*	
Chaffinch	*Fringilla coelebs*	
Crow, Carrion	*Corvus corone*	
Dipper	*Cinclus cinclus*	
Dunnock	*Prunella modularis*	
Greenfinch	*Carduelis chloris*	
Heron, Grey	*Ardea cinerea*	
Jackdaw	*Corvus monedula*	
Lapwing	*Vanellus vanellus*	
Robin	*Erithacus rubecula*	
Rook	*Corvus frugilegus*	

English name	Latin name	Dates on which seen
Sparrow, House	*Passer domesticus*	
Starling	*Sturnus vulgaris*	
Thrush, Song	*Turdus philomelos*	
Tit, Blue	*Parus caeruleus*	
Coal	*ater*	
Great	*major*	
Long-tailed	*Aegithalos caudatus*	
Treecreeper	*Certhia familiaris*	
Wagtail, Grey	*Motacilla cinerea*	
Pied	*alba*	
Wren	*Troglodytes troglodytes*	

Summer visitors

Blackcap	*Sylvia atricapilla*	
Flycatcher, Spotted	*Muscicapa striata*	
Warbler, Garden	*Sylvia boris*	
Willow	*Phylloscopus trochilus*	
Whitethroat	*Sylvia communis*	

Other birds seen

Walk 6 — Cramond Shore and Wooded Valley of the Almond

English name	Latin name	Dates on which seen
Residents		
Blackbird	*Turdus merula*	
Blackcap	*Sylvia atricapilla*	
Chaffinch	*Fringilla coelebs*	
Coot	*Fulica atra*	
Crow, Carrion	*Corvus corone*	
Curlew	*Numenius arquata*	

English name	Latin name	Dates on which seen
Dipper	*Cinclus cinclus*	
Dunlin	*Calidris alpina*	
Flycatcher, Spotted	*Muscicapa striata*	
Godwit, Bar-tailed	*Limosa lapponica*	
Goldcrest	*Regulus regulus*	
Gull, Black-headed	*Larus ridibundus*	
Common	*canus*	
Great Black-backed	*marinus*	
Herring	*argentatus*	
Lesser Black-backed	*fuscus*	
Heron, Grey	*Ardea cinerea*	
Knot	*Calidris canutus*	
Mallard	*Anas platyrhynchos*	
Moorhen	*Gallinula chloropus*	
Oystercatcher	*Haematopus ostralegus*	
Plover, Golden	*Pluvialis apricaria*	
Ringed	*Charadrius hiaticula*	
Redshank	*Tringa totanus*	
Robin	*Erithacus rubecula*	
Shelduck	*Tadorna tadorna*	
Starling	*Sturnus vulgaris*	
Swan, Mute	*Cygnus olor*	
Tern, Arctic	*Sterna paradisaea*	
Common	*hirundo*	
Sandwich	*sandvicensis*	
Thrush, Mistle	*Turdus viscivorus*	
Song	*philomelos*	
Tit, Blue	*Parus caeruleus*	
Great	*major*	
Treecreeper	*Certhia familiaris*	
Turnstone	*Arenaria interpres*	
Wagtail, Grey	*Motacilla cinerea*	
Pied	*alba*	

English name	Latin name	Dates on which seen
Warbler, Garden	*Sylvia borin*	
Willow	*Phylloscopus trochilus*	
Wren	*Troglodytes troglodytes*	

Other birds seen

Water birds seen at Duddingston

English name	Latin name	Dates on which seen
Coot	*Fulica atra*	
Cormorant	*Phalacrocorax carbo*	
Duck, Tufted	*Aythya fuligula*	
Goldeneye	*Bucephala clangula*	
Goose, Canada	*Branta canadensis*	
Greylag	*Anser anser*	
Grebe, Great Crested	*Podiceps cristatus*	
Little	*Tachybaptus ruficollis*	
Heron, Grey	*Ardea cinera*	
Mallard	*Anas platyrhynchos*	
Moorhen	*Gallinula chloropus*	
Pochard	*Aythya ferina*	
Shoveler	*Anas clypeata*	
Swan, Mute	*Cygnus olor*	
Teal	*Anas crecca*	
Wigeon	*Anas penelope*	

Other birds seen

Seabirds and Waders seen from Leith Docks and Seafield

English name	Latin name	Dates on which seen
Cormorant	*Phalacrocorax carbo*	
Curlew	*Numenius arquata*	
Dunlin	*Calidris alpina*	
Eider	*Somateria mollissima*	
Fulmar	*Fulmaris glacialis*	
Gannet	*Sula bassana*	
Godwit, Bar-tailed	*Limosa lapponica*	
Goldeneye	*Bucephala clangula*	
Grebe, Great Crested	*Podiceps cristatus*	
Gull, Black-headed	*Larus ridibundus*	
Common	*canus*	
Great Black-backed	*marinus*	
Herring	*argentatus*	
Lesser Black-backed	*fuscus*	
Kittiwake	*Rissa tridactyla*	
Knot	*Calidris canutus*	
Mallard	*Anas platyrhynchos*	
Merganser, Red-breasted	*Mergus serrator*	
Oystercatcher	*Haematopus ostralegus*	
Plover, Ringed	*Charadrius hiaticula*	
Redshank	*Tringa totanus*	
Scaup	*Aythya marila*	
Skua, Arctic	*Stercorarius parasiticus*	
Tern, Artic	*Sterna paradisaea*	
Common	*hirundo*	
Sandwich	*sandvicensis*	
Turnstone	*Arenaria interpres*	

Other birds seen

Reference books

Flowering Plants (including trees)

Ary, S. and Gregory, M. *The Oxford Book of Wild Flowers.* Oxford U. P., London, 1960.

Christiansen, M. S. *Grasses, Sedges and Rushes.* Blandford, Poole, 1979.

Clapham, A. R., Tutin, T. G. and Warburg. E. F. *Excursion Flora of the British Isles.* Cambridge U. P. (Basic work for identification), Cambridge, 1959.

Fitter, R. S. F., Fitter, A. and Blamey, M. *The Wild Flowers of Britain and Northern Europe,* Collins, London, 1974.

Hubbard, C. E. *Grasses.* Penguin, Harmondsworth, 1954.

McClintock, D. and Fitter, R. S. F. *The Pocket Guide to Wild Flowers,* Collins, London, 1956.

Martin, W. K. *The Concise British Flora in Colour.* Ebury Press, London, 1965.

Rose, F., *The Wild Flower Key*, Warne, London, 1981.

Trees

Edlin, H. L., *The Tree Key,* Warne, London, 1978.

HMSO. *Know Your Broadleaves*, Forestry Commission Booklet No. 20, London, 1968.

HMSO. *Know Your Conifers.* Foresrtry Commission Booklet No. 15, London, 1970.

Phillips, R. *Trees in Britain Europe and North America.* Pan Books, London, 1978.

Polunin, O. *Trees and Bushes of Britain and Europe.* Paladin, St Albans, 1977.

Rushforth, K. *The Mitchell Beazley Pocket guide to Trees.* Mitchell Beazley, London, 1980.

Flowerless Plants

General

Brightman, F. H. and Nicholson, B. L. *The Oxford Book of Flowerless Plants (ferns, fungi, mosses and liverworts, lichens and seaweeds),* Oxford U. P., London, 1965.

Phillips, R. *Grasses*, Ferns, Mosses and Lichens,* Pan Books, London, 1980.
(*flowering plants).

Fungi

Lange, M. and Hora, F. B. *Collins Guide to Mushrooms and Toadstools,* Collins, London, 1963.

Nilsson, S. and Persson, O. *Fungi of Northern Europe, Books 1 and 2,* Penguin, Harmondsworth, 1978.

Phillips, R., *Mushrooms,* Pan Books, London, 1981.

Lichens

Alvin, K. L. *The Observers Book of Lichens,* Warne, London, 1977.

Invertebrates

General

Barrett, J. and Yonge, C. M. *Collins Pocket Guide to the Sea Shore,* Collins, London, 1958.

Clegg, J. ed. *Pond and Stream Life in Colour,* Blandford, Poole, 1963.

Darlington, A. *The Pocket Encyclopaedia of Plant Galls,* Blandford, Poole, 1968.

Nichols, D., Cooke, J. A. L. and Whitely, D. *The Oxford Book of Invertebrates: protozoa, sponges, coelenterates, worms, molluscs, echinoderms and arthropods (other than insects).* Oxford U. P., London, 1971.

Insects

Chinery. M. *A Field Guide to the Insects of Britain and Northern Europe,* Collins, London, 1973.

Ford, R. L. E. *The Observer's Book of Larger Moths,* Warne, London, 1974.

Goodden, R. *British Butterflies. A Field Guide*. David & Charles, Newton Abbot, 1978.

Higgins, L. G. and Riley, N. D. *A Field Guide to Butterflies of Britain and Europe*, Collins, London, 1970.

Shells
McMillan, N. F. *The Observer's Book of Seashells of the British Isles,* Warne, London, 1977.

Vertebrates

General
Bang, P. and Dahlstrom, P. *Collins Guide to Animal Tracks and Signs*, Collins, London, 1974.

Reptiles and amphibia
Hvass, H. *Reptiles and Amphibians*, Blandford, Poole, 1972.

Birds
Fitter, R, S. F. and Richardson, P. S. *Pocket Guide to British Birds,* Collins, London, 1952.

Hayman, P. *R.S.P.B. Birdwatcher's Pocket Guide,* Mitchell Beazley, London, 1952.

Peterson, P., Mountford, G. and Hollom, P. H. *A Field Guide to the Birds of Britain and Europe*, Collins, London, 1954.

Mammals
Brink, H. van der. *A Field Guide to the Mammals of Britain and Europe*, Collins, London, 1967.

Corbet, G. B. and Ovenden. D. *The Mammals of Britain and Europe*, Collins, London, 1980.

Lawrence, M. J. and Brown, R. W. *Mammals of Britain*. Blandford, Poole, 1967.

Lyneborg, R. *Mammals in Colour*. Blandford, Poole, 1971.

Geology

Black, G. P. *Arthur's Seat: a history of Edinburgh's volcano,* Oliver & Boyd, Edinburgh, 1966.

Craig, G. Y. and Duff, P. McL. D. eds. *The Geology of the Lothians and South-East Scotland—An Excursion Guide*. Scottish Academic Press, Edinburgh, 1975.

Evans, I. O. *The Observer's Book of Geology*. Warne, London, 1949.

For Further Reading

Burton, M. ed. *The Shell Natural History of Britain.* Michael Joseph, London, 1970.

Chinery, M. *The Natural History of the Garden.* Collins, London, 1977.

HMSO. *The Story of the Earth.* Geological Museum, London, 1972.

HMSO. *Volcanoes.* Geological Museum, London, 1974.

Owen, D. F. *What is Ecology?* Oxford U.P., London, 1974.

Reade, W. and Stuttard, R. M. *A Handbook for Naturalists.* Evans Bros Ltd., London, 1968.

Soper, T. *Wildlife Begins at Home.* David & Charles, Newton Abbot, 1975.

Southwood, T. R. E. *Life of the Wayside and Woodland.* Warne, London, 1923.

Tansley, A. G. *Britain's Green Mantle.* George Allen & Unwin Ltd., London, 1949.

Country Code

Please remember to use the Country Code on your walks and on making visits. Leave the Edinburgh countryside for others who come after you to enjoy.

1. Guard against all risk of fire.
2. Fasten all gates.
3. Keep dogs under proper control.
4. Keep to paths across farmland.
5. Avoid damaging fencing, hedges and walls.
6. Leave no litter.
7. Protect wildlife, wild plants and trees.
8. Safeguard water supplies.
9. Go carefully on country roads.
10. Respect the life of the countryside.

Reference books used

Anderson, M. L., *A History of Scottish Forestry*, 1962

Black, G. P., *Arthur's Seat: a history of Edinburgh's volcano,* 1966

City of Edinburgh District Council Planning Department, *Water of Leith Walkway pamphlets, Balerno to Juniper Green, Slateford to Juniper Green*

Clare, R., Rocks and Landscape, 1972

Edinburgh Education Department, *Nature Trail Booklet, Hermitage of Braid — Blackford*

Edinburgh Geological Society, *The Geology of the Lothians and South East Scotland; an excursion guide*, 1975

Grant, J., *Old and new Edinburgh: its history, people and places*, 1880

Journals of the Edinburgh Natural History Society, 1965-1977

McLaren, M., *Shell Guide to Scotland*, 1965

Napier College of Commerce and Technology, *Holyrood Park project, 1977-1978*

Newey, W. W., *Pollen analysis from south east Scotland, Transactions of Botanical Society of Edinburgh, Vol. 40, part IV*, 1968

Pennington, W., *The History of British Vegetation*, 1974

Third Statistical Account of Scotland: The City of Edinburgh, 1966

Youngson, A. J., *The making of classical Edinburgh*, 1966

Addresses

The Carnegie UK Trust
Comely Park House
Dunfermline
Fife KY12 7EJ

Edinburgh Natural History Society
Hon Sec Mrs C. Stewart
41 Craigleith Hill Avenue
Edinburgh EH4 2JL

Botanical Society of Edinburgh (B.S.E.)
c/o Royal Botanic Garden
Inverleith Row
Edinburgh 3

Council for Environmental Conservation (Co En Co)
Zoological Gardens
Regent's Park
London NW1 4RY

Edinburgh Geological Society
c/o The Honorary Secretary
Grant Institute of Geological Sciences
West Mains Road
Edinburgh EH9 3JW

National Trust for Scotland
5 Charlotte Square
Edinburgh EH2 4DU

Nature Conservancy Council
12 Hope Terrace
Edinburgh EA9 2AS

Royal Society for Nature Conservation
The Green
Nettleham
Lincoln LN2 2NR

Royal Scottish Museum
Chambers Street
Edinburgh 1

Royal Society for the Protection of Birds (Scotland) (R.S.P.B.)
17 Regent Terrace
Edinburgh EH7 5BN

Scottish Ornithologists' Club (S.O.C.)
21 Regent Terrace
Edinburgh EH7 5BN

Scottish Wildlife Trust (S.W.T.)
25 Johnston Terrace
Edinburgh EH1 2NH